CREATING
YOUR OWN
MONOLOGUE

Glenn Alterman

ALLWORTH PRESS
NEW YORK

04 03 02 01 00 99   5 4 3 2 1

Published by Allworth Press
An imprint of Allworth Communications, Inc.
10 East 23rd Street, New York, NY 10010

Cover design by Douglas Design Associates, New York, NY
Page composition/typography by SR Desktop Services, Ridge, NY

ISBN: 1-58115-038-5

Library of Congress Cataloging-in-Publication Data
Alterman, Glenn, 1946–
    Creating your own monologue / by Glenn Alterman.
        p.   cm.
    Includes index.
    ISBN 1-58115-038-5 (PBK.)
    1. Monologue—Authorship.   2. Performance art—Authorship.
    3. Monodramas—Authorship.   4. Acting—Auditions.   5. Playwriting.
    I. Title.
    PN1530.A48   1999
    808.2'45—dc21   99-048073

Printed in Canada

DEDICATION

I dedicate this book to all solo performers who have ever had
the courage to stand alone on a stage and perform their own material.

I also dedicate this book to every monologist whose work has inspired me
to create my own monologues and to write this book.

CONTENTS

What Is a Monologue?
Types of Monologues
What Is Performance Art?

Samuel Foote (1721–1777) Creates the One-Person Show
George Alexander Stevens, the Father of the Monologue
Charles Mathews
Ruth Draper Perfects the Monologue
Cornelia Otis Skinner
Historical Monologues
The Solo Show Today

Questions to Ask Yourself Before Starting Work on a Solo Show
The Similarities/Differences between Being an Actor and Working As a Writer
As an Actor, Do I Have the Necessary Skills to Create My Own Material?
Pluses and Minuses, Assessing Specifically Where You Are Now
Your Sense of Truth

Writing
What Is Creative Writing?
Fear of Writing
Journal Writing
Using a Tape Recorder
Improvising: "Are You Talkin' to Me?"
Working Orally: In Front of an Audience
Working Orally: Developing Your Stories throughout the Day

ACKNOWLEDGMENTS

I wish to thank: Kathleen Russo (Washington Square Arts), Seth Gordon, Abigail McGrath, Doug Barron (Plaza Desk Top Publishing), Andre DeShields, David Pace, Greg Phillips (CSTAR—Creative Stage Artists Management), Eleanor Speert, and Nicole Potter.

INTRODUCTION

I am an actor; I have been for over thirty years. About twelve years ago, I became a writer, more specifically, a monologue writer. How? Why? Well, like many actors, I was constantly looking for new monologues for auditions. It was a tiresome process. Each monologue that I'd find seemed to have something wrong with it, something that eliminated it from my being able to use it for auditions. Some were overused, some were too long and couldn't be cut (and keep the story cohesive), others were too reliant on the plays they came from, others . . . well it went on and on. It was a very frustrating situation, to say the least. I was constantly monologue hunting when I could have been better spending my time looking for acting work.

Basically what I was looking for in a monologue was something that I could hook into, a monologue that had a story that engaged me, characters that touched me, a situation that interested me. I must have logged in hundreds of hours over the years looking for that one perfect monologue. On the rare occasion that I found one that I could use, I'd do it so often that it would become stale in no time, and I'd be back once again looking through monologue books and plays trying to find another one.

One day, on a whim, well actually out of total frustration, I decided to bite the bullet and try to write one myself. Considering that I'd never written creatively before, I knew it was going to be a challenge. After all those years of monologue hunting, I certainly knew what I wanted. The monologue that I was going to write would have a beginning, middle, and end; a conflict of some kind; and a character that interested me and with whom I could identify. But most importantly, it had to have a good yarn, an engaging story.

It was trial and error for quite a while; lots of looking at the walls, throwing crumpled sheets of paper into the wastebasket. But one thing I gradually began to realize was that I could use my acting skills to help me write monologues. Some of the same skills that I'd used as an actor to create characters in plays, I also could use to create characters in monologues. After a few very long, trying weeks, I completed my first monologue. I felt a tremendous sense of achievement. This was something I had never done before. I had now become a monologue writer! There was nothing left to do but try it out, see if the monologue worked.

I was studying acting at that time with Wynn Handman in New York. I brought my new monologue to class one night and nervously performed it. It went over very well. Everyone wanted to know where I had found this great new monologue. After confessing that I'd written it, about five or six actors asked if I'd write one for them. I agreed to, and began writing monologues almost every day after that. The more I wrote, the more I realized I was on to something. I started to develop a more efficient way of working. Over the next few months, I turned out a lot of monologues. That's not to say that every one of them was a gem, no, not at all. Actually, there were more flops than hits. But I learned more from my mistakes than from my successes. On any given night in Wynn Handman's class, I'd have up to three new monologues being performed by different actors for the first time. At the end of that first year, I had completed nearly eighty monologues (not to mention the dozens of discarded ones). Each night in class when the monologues were read, I was always open to any comments, any criticism, that anyone had. I took notes, kept records, and created a file. Over the years, that file has grown extensively. It is the basis for my monologue classes as well as this book.

Since writing that first monologue over twelve years ago, I've written several hundred monologues, had four successful books of monologues published, and had dozens of my monologue plays performed all over the country. In my classes, I've seen actors, who never thought they could write, suddenly develop into skilled and successful monologists. I've written this book for actors, actors who are fed up and tired of spending countless hours looking through plays and monologue books for that one perfect piece.

Over the past twelve years, as I have honed my skills as a writer, the American theater has experienced a resurgence of interest in the one-person show. Coming out of diverse backgrounds and disciplines, many artists today are creating and performing full-length solo works. Obviously these appeal to presenting organizations in part because of economics; it is usually much cheaper to produce one actor on a bare stage than to mount a lavish musical. But clearly, these producers would not continue to present solo shows if the audience didn't support them. Perhaps these performances appeal to viewers because they often permit an intimacy that is missing from other forms of entertainment. Perhaps they are popular because they showcase the virtuosity and versatility of the actor, attributes that can disappear in the sauce of special effects and editing that comprise other popular media. Perhaps solo shows captivate audiences because they contain such clear, quirky, and individual worldviews.

This book is also intended for actors who are seriously thinking of creating their own one-person shows. As you will notice in the monologist interview section, the artists I interviewed have many different points of view, many different reasons for needing to speak their minds. Quite a few were frustrated actors who, tired of waiting for their phones to ring, decided to take matters in their own hands and create their own shows. Once that decision was reached, the roads that these performers took in building and shaping their own material were almost as diverse as the artists themselves. But all of them had to go through the process of discovering what they wanted to say and how they were going to say it.

I hope this book will guide you in finding a working method that clicks for you and ultimately results in a finished piece. I've tried to cover every possible aspect of creating your own monologue, and I have included sections on marketing and performance venues for your finished piece. I think that you'll find the interview sections with the solo artists and directors helpful, inspiring, and informative.

A final side note: In writing this book, my editor and I struggled to find an appropriate and inoffensive way to use pronouns. Since "he/she" is awkward and "them" is incorrect, we have settled, in the main, on pairing "the actor" or "the writer" with forms of the third-person masculine pronoun "he." Although this may be considered gender biased, it was my editor's feeling that we should sacrifice political correctness for the sake of simplicity and clarity.

I'm not saying that writing your own monologue will be easy, but I can almost guarantee that if you can commit to it, it can be an incredibly empowering and artistically satisfying experience.

—GLENN ALTERMAN
December 31, 1998
New York City

Six Ways to Get
the Most out of This Book

1. I suggest, at first, that you *don't* read this book nonstop from cover to cover.
2. The best way to get the most value out of this book is to first look through the table of contents, then skim through the book, stopping at particular chapters that you feel are pertinent to the monologue that you're presently writing or thinking about writing.
3. Next, I suggest that you read through the entire book, taking notes on whatever you feel will help you specifically with what you're working on or about to work on.
4. Once you have begun work on your monologue, I suggest that you occasionally refer back to the chapters dealing with process: "Starting to Write," "Beginning Your Monologue: Structure and Process," "Developing Your Monologue," and so on.
5. Reread some of the excerpts by the monologists used to illustrate points in this book. You may find their material helpful, informative, and inspiring.
6. In addition to the monologue excerpts in this book, it's always helpful when working on monologues to browse through material from other monologists or writers whom you respect. Their work may be a source of inspiration during difficult periods.

A Definition of Terms

For our purpose in this book, solo art refers to one actor/artist, alone on a stage before a live audience, performing material that he has created.

What Is a Monologue?

Webster defines a monologue as "a dramatic soliloquy" and as "a long speech." In a play, a monologue is an uninterrupted speech. Monologues can be quite flexible as to the form they take. Some monologues are delivered directly to the audience. Some try to create the impression that the actor is alone, talking to himself. Other monologues occur when the actor (in character) is talking to an imaginary person (or people). When speaking to an imaginary person, the character may be saying things that he always wanted to say but didn't get the chance, or didn't have the courage to say, or perhaps is preparing to say. In many, if not most, audition monologues, the actor (in character) is speaking to another character. The actor is imagining the other character and his responses. An example of this would be Linda Loman's "Attention Must Be Paid" monologue from *Death of a Salesman*. In this case, Linda is actually speaking to her sons, even if the actress is imagining them on the back wall.

The short monologue generally runs from two to ten minutes. It has a relatively uncomplicated story with not too many characters. Successful short monologues are highly condensed experiences that can be thought of as the theater's equivalent to poetry. Generally, these monologues are written for auditions, acting-class work, or to be a part of a larger play of multiple monologues. Casting directors and agents pride themselves on their ability to make snap judgments, so when you write for auditions, it is best to remember that brevity is the soul of wit. An audition piece that unfolds slowly will still be folded when the agent says "thank you." For this strange format, your material ought not to exceed three minutes.

A long monologue or monodrama is a one-person play. Monodramas can be a powerful form of theater. Quite often, the writer uses elevated language and strong images to create a poetic enlargement of the characters and subject.

Monodramas are like all plays in that they have a beginning, middle, and end; contain concise dialogue; and express the writer's personal vision. They vary as to style, content, and time. What make monodramas so exciting and challenging to work on are the flexible forms they can take. Although there is only one actor on stage, he can bring many characters into the piece by assuming their personalities and voices. Although many monodramas incorporate conflict, it's not always necessary. The writer can rely on interesting characters, choice of words (dialogue), a dramatic situation, and so on to make his piece theatrical.

Types of Monologues

It's difficult to categorize monologues and monodramas because, quite often, they are hybrids of style. The following categories are somewhat arbitrary but hopefully will be of some use in identifying specific characteristics of both monologues and monologue plays.

AUTOBIOGRAPHICAL NARRATIVE MONOLOGUES

In these plays, the artist recalls actual stories and events from his life. The actor/writer generally is the narrator in these pieces. There may be little or no attempt to perform different characters in the story. The emphasis here is on the telling of his tale. Spalding Gray's monologue, *Swimming to Cambodia,* is an example of this mainly narrative storytelling style (see interview). In *Swimming to Cambodia,* Gray recalls his fascinating experiences while working as an actor during the making of the movie *The Killing Fields.*

Another example of an autobiographical monologue is Evan Handler's *Time on Fire* (see interview). In his play, Mr. Handler tells the story of a time in his life when he was dealing with a life threatening cancer. His story reveals the helplessness patients quite often feel when dealing with medical bureaucracy.

AUTOBIOGRAPHICAL CHARACTER MONOLOGUES

Some autobiographical monologue plays are character driven, relying mainly on dialogue rather than narrative. The actor/writer acts out his story with multiple characters to propel the story.

Chaz Palminteri's *A Bronx Tale* is a play based on his recollections of growing up in the Bronx. At the age of thirty-six, Palminteri wrote and performed this thirty-five–character one-man show that was a major success and was later turned into a film starring Robert De Niro (and many other actors).

CHARACTER-DRIVEN, FICTIONAL MONOLOGUES

In these plays, the actor/writer creates multiple characters to either express a theme, display a lifestyle, or to tell a (sometimes) imaginary story. In many cases, the characters have a common connection. For instance, John Leguizamo's plays (*Freak, Spic-O-Rama, Mambo Mouth*) are generally about Latin characters. Many of his characters are based on family members and people from the neighborhood in which he grew up.

Danny Hoch portrays mainly urban characters, many living on the edge, in his character monologues (see interview).

Sometimes one character acts as the spine of the piece. In Lily Tomlin's *The Search for Intelligent Life*, Trudy, a mad bag lady, serves as a narrator who has befriended aliens from outer space who have come to study a "planet in puberty." Tomlin inhabited twenty-four characters during the course of her play.

REALITY-BASED DOCU-MONOLOGUES

These pieces are created from real-life events. The monologist uses the exact words of the people who were involved. In her play *Twilight: Los Angeles, 1992*, Anna Deavere Smith relates the experiences of forty-six characters in the wake of the Rodney King verdict and the riots that followed. Ms. Smith portrayed all of the characters. She obtained her information by tape-recording the actual people and taking notes on their speech tics and vocal inflections. For more information on reality-based docu-monologue, see Christopher Ashley's interview later on in the book. (He was Ms. Smith's director in her play *Fires in the Mirror.*)

TOPICAL MONOLOGUES

These monologues rely heavily on the events of the day as seen through the eyes of the monologist. They are part autobiographical, part observation, and part opinion. There is a thin line between topical monologues and stand-up comedy. Both generally incorporate anecdotes, jokes, and personal observations. I feel however that there are differences between the two. For one thing, the topical monologist's intention isn't only to get laughs from his material. His stories generally have a wider sweep, and generally there is more of a cohesive quality to his piece. Stand-up comics primarily tell jokes, although, on occasion, they will also include some anecdotal material. Kate Clinton's funny, feminist topical monologues express her particular view of the world as she sees it (see interview and excerpt). She has done both stand-up and theatrical topical monologues.

STORYTELLING MONOLOGUES

These are fictional stories performed by the actor/writer. They are generally written in narrative form, in which the actor serves as storyteller. During the telling of the story, the actor will occasionally break the narrative form to momentarily become one of the characters, and then immediately return to the narrator-storyteller role. *St. Nicholas* by Conor McPhearson is an excellent example of this form. In this monologue play, a fictitious character tells an intriguing imaginary tale of vampires and late-night debauchery.

What Is Performance Art?

An agreed upon meaning of the term "performance art" is very difficult to find. Unlike the word "monologue," there is no dictionary definition. Performance art can be described as an expression of an artist's creativity through visual art, drama, multimedia, dance, or music. Performance art is to theater what poetry is to prose. I asked several solo artists and directors of solo shows how they would define performance art.

Director Jo Bonney said, "The label 'performance art' has always been applied to things that are illusive and flexible. The very term 'performance art' actually came out of the visual arts scene. Artists were creating happenings. These happenings usually took place in galleries. They took place in real time. They generally were a way an artist could explore something, a concept, a visual idea. They were not just for some entertainment value, to entertain an audience. They were generally attended by members of the art community. Basically what I'm saying is that 'performance art' is just a label. It seems that many artists who come out of a theater background don't choose to use that label for their work. Dancers, cabaret performers, visual artists tend to use it more often to describe and identify their work. But basically it's a very illusive term."

Penny Arcade, a performance artist, asserts, "My work is a combination, I suppose, of very personal and very political, which is in a sense, performance art. It's hard to say where one ends and the other begins."

Dael Orlandersmith defines a performance artist as "someone who technically breaks the fourth wall with the audience. It's a form of storytelling that relies heavily on the audience in some way."

Because of the amorphous definition and the variety of forms that performance art pieces can take, it's difficult to provide general guidelines for approaching them. In this book, for simplicity and clarity I will mainly be dealing with the textual aspects of performance art pieces. For a more in-depth discussion of creating performance art, I refer you to such books as *The Art of Performance, a Critical Anthology*, edited by Battcock, Gregory, Nickas, and Roberts. This book offers a fascinating collection of essays by performance artists as well as by established critics of performance art.

A Brief History of the One-Person Show

Most people believe that the one-man show is a recent phenomenon that started here in America. They might be surprised to learn that it actually began back in the eighteenth century.

Samuel Foote (1721–1777) Creates the One-Person Show

Samuel Foote was a British satirist. Foote wrote *The Rehearsal,* a burlesque, in which he mimicked some of the political figures and well-known actors of the day. *The Rehearsal* was an extremely popular theatrical piece.

In April of 1747, Foote opened a new play, *The Diversions of the Morning.* I should mention that originally Foote's shows were not totally solo. There were other actors on the stage with him. But it was primarily his solo work as a mimic that audiences enjoyed most. Foote continued his solo satires for the next thirty years. His plays at times could be quite offensive. Nevertheless, they were the "must-see" for the audiences of his day.

Over the years, there were many others who followed in Foote's tradition of solo mimicry. Among those most famous were George Saville Carey, who was famous for his impersonations of other actors, and Harry Woodward, a comedian who wrote solo topical skits.

George Alexander Stevens, the Father of the Monologue

It wasn't until 1764, when George Alexander Stevens wrote *Lecture upon Heads*, that the monologue as an art form truly came into being. By all accounts, Stevens's monologue ran about two hours. During the monologue, he poked fun at many things, but mostly at many of the great statesmen of the day. He also lampooned common stereotypes and social behavior. Stevens's shows were a major success and had very long runs (nearly a thousand performances each).

Stevens's success opened the floodgates for copycats, spin-offs, and imitators. These imitations were not just limited to England. Quite a few other countries, including America, had their own versions of Stevens's *Lecture upon Heads*. The copyright laws at that time were very limited and could not protect his work.

Charles Mathews

During the nineteenth century, Charles Mathews, a comic actor and mimic, wrote *The Mail Coach Adventure*, which later evolved into what became his very popular one-man show. Eventually Mathews developed an entire group of solo shows called *At Homes*, which he toured in both England and America. Like Foote's monologues, Mathews's monologues mimicked many of the famous actors of the day, but unlike Foote's, Mathews's were not offensive.

By the early 1900s, monologues were quite often used to "cover" while scenery was being changed during a play. Also, if some minor technical disaster occurred during a play's performance, the monologist would be out in front keeping the audience entertained. Today's warm-up entertainers do a similar job both before and during the taping of sitcoms and late-night audience shows.

Ruth Draper Perfects the Monologue

Perhaps one of the most famous monologists of all time was Ruth Draper. Draper, an actress, performed many of her one-woman shows during the 1920s, 1930s, and 1940s. Her first show of "monos" as she called them, was performed in England in 1920. The two-hour-long evening was composed of an assortment of well-developed characters created totally from her imagination. From the very beginning, the critics raved about her work as a monologist. She spoke many languages and performed her monologues all over the world.

Draper's characters ranged from the very poor to the extremely wealthy, and they had a true-to-life quality to them. Through her characters, she developed her monos into mini plays with a beginning, middle, and end. She never used a script but relied totally on her memory. Her characters were constantly changing and evolving. She was never content with her work and was always looking for new ways to express herself. She tried to work as simply as possible, without too much clutter. A prop as simple as a hat or a handbag was all that was required. Add to that a chair and a table and she was ready to create magic, "Draper's magic" as it was called. She had a tremendous belief in the actor's ability to pretend. She felt that if she truly committed herself to her imagination in creating her characters, the audience would believe in them.

Cornelia Otis Skinner

A contemporary and admirer of Draper was Cornelia Otis Skinner. When Skinner first began performing her one-woman shows, there were many similarities between her work and Draper's. Eventually, however, her taste ran toward more sumptuous costume dramas. In 1937, she performed an adaptation of *Edna, His Wife*, a best-selling novel of the day. This further distinguished her from Draper, who primarily did "character-created plays." Skinner also made a very comfortable living as an actress in regular plays, and was a well-respected writer and essayist.

Historical Monologues

As I mentioned earlier, solo shows went through a period of decline, but historical solo shows continued being popular even during that period. Some monologists created shows based on real rather than imaginary characters. Emlyn Williams played Charles Dickens, Paul Shyre played H. L. Mencken, James Whitmore performed in *Will Rogers U.S.A.,* and Hal Holbrook was *Mark Twain Tonight!* These are just a few that come to mind.

Some solo plays have been written for specific actors by playwrights. Samuel Beckett wrote *Krapp's Last Tape* for Patrick Magee; Cocteau wrote *Le Fantome de Marseille* for Edith Piaf; William Luce wrote *The Belle of Amherst* for Julie Harris.

The Solo Show Today

On Broadway there have been many successful one-person shows. Rob Becker's *Defending the Caveman* presently holds the record for the longest running one-man show on Broadway. Becker wrote his piece specifically for himself and developed it around the country at different comedy clubs before bringing it to New York.

Another successful one-person Broadway show was *Shirley Valentine* with Pauline Collins. This play about a lonely housewife and her imaginary world was written for Ms. Collins by playwright Willy Russell and won her the Tony for best actress in 1989. In 1986, Lily Tomlin was awarded a Tony for best actress for her one-woman show, *The Search for Intelligent Life in the Universe.* Alec McGowan was nominated for a Tony in 1979 for his reading of *The Gospel According St. Mark.*

Sherry Glaser's *Family Secrets,* presently the longest playing off-Broadway solo show, is about five interconnected male and female family members, all played by Miss Glaser (see interview).

Eric Bogosian, Laurie Anderson, Danny Hoch (see interview), Anna Deavere Smith, Spalding Gray (see interview), and John Leguizamo are just a few of today's many solo artists who have made very successful careers for themselves with their solo work.

There are probably more monologists and solo artists performing their work today than ever. Because of the high cost of regular play productions, solo shows are welcomed in many regional theaters, as well as off-Broadway and on Broadway. It seems like every Broadway season now has at least one solo show.

If you are interested in a more detailed history of one-person shows, I highly recommend *Acting Solo: The Art of One-Man Shows,* by Jordan R. Young (Moonstone Press, 1989). I personally found this book to be an excellent source for the research that I did on this subject .

A PRELIMINARY LOOK

think that it's very important before you begin work to ask yourself, "Exactly why am I doing this?" Obviously the answer is going to be different if your intention is to write a short monologue for auditions than if you're planning to commit yourself to writing a solo show. If you are planning to write your audition piece, it may well be because you are frustrated with the material that is out there, and you think you can showcase yourself better than a playwright who doesn't know you or your special talents. Audition pieces have specific guidelines that you will probably want to abide by, mainly in terms of length and arc. I will deal with the particular demands of the short/audition monologue in a discrete chapter, but in general, most of what I have to say about creating a solo show can be applied to a short monologue as well.

If you are thinking about creating a solo show, you, like many of the actors interviewed in this book, may have decided, out of frustration and unemployment, "Hell with them, I'll write my own show and star in it!" You will learn, as they did, that creating your own show requires a tremendous amount of work. If your only reason for writing is to provide yourself with an acting job, perhaps you should consider what's ahead of you. The commitment level for writing a solo show is quite extensive. There's a tremendous amount of work involved. Some solo shows can take many months, even years, to complete.

Questions to Ask Yourself
Before Starting Work on a Solo Show

- Am I really committed to doing this?
- Am I willing to work on this for however long it takes?
- I realize that I'll be alone on stage for each performance. Can I handle that responsibility and pressure?
- Do I believe that I have the talent to keep an audience entertained for up to two hours?
- If I chose to use my own experience as the basis for the show, what do I want to share with the audience?
- Are there painful or funny stories from my life that I want to reveal to the world?
- If I'm planning on writing character monologues, do I feel that I'm a versatile enough performer to carry them off with variety, allowing for each character to be fully realized?
- If I don't have the technical skills now (dialects, etc.), am I willing to work as hard as I can to develop them while working on my show?

If, after answering all these questions, you are willing to commit yourself to all the work involved in creating your own solo show, all I have to say is congratulations, welcome aboard! I'll do the best that I can to help you find the answers to questions that inevitably will come up along the way. At this point my only advice is:

- Try to stay focused on what you're doing.
- Keep your goal constantly in mind.
- If it gets uncomfortable, even frustrating at times, don't give up; just work through it.

The Similarities/Differences between Being an Actor and Working As a Writer

The most obvious similarities between the actor and the writer is that both are creative artists and both use their imagination in their work. That ability to use your imagination as an actor will be very helpful in the work we'll be doing here.

Generally, the actor interprets and performs what the writer/playwright has written. The interdependence of both professions should be obvious. However, the actor's creative life involves constant collaboration with other artists (the director, other actors, etc.) early on in a play's production. The writer generally does his initial creating alone. After he's written the play, he collaborates with the production team (producer, director, actors, etc.). Since this book offers guidance for actors in creating their own material, we'll be looking at techniques and approaches that merge both of these professions.

As you will note, in the interview section, not all actors/creators work as the traditional writer does, although some do adhere to a more "writerly" process.

As an Actor, Do I Have the Necessary Skills to Create My Own Material?

I personally feel that anyone can write, tell stories, create monologues. If you've lived and had experiences, then you have stories like no one else. Your stories are unique, yours and yours alone. How you'll tell your stories is as individual as you are. No one else has lived your life or knows the things that you've seen or felt.

- The secret to writing *autobiographical monologues* is learning how to access your private stories, your memories, your point of view, and put them into words.
- The creation of fictional *character monologues* requires keen observation of people, a good ear for dialogue, and a healthy imagination.
- *Performance art pieces* require a commitment to a purely personal vision, a good imagination, and, quite often, a variety of performance skills.

As I've mentioned, actors interpret and perform what writers have written. As an actor, if you've worked on plays, you're already familiar with all the ingredients of playwriting, character, dialogue, scenes, drama, comedy, etc. Therefore, it's safe to assume that you already have some basic knowledge of the mechanics of playwriting, and more importantly, of character development. Writing your own material may not be as difficult or as complicated as you imagined. It's much like going through to the other side of the mirror. Now, instead of being merely the instrument of a writer's vision, you will create the world that you're going to inhabit, perform, play in.

Pluses and Minuses, Assessing Specifically Where You Are Now

It's helpful here at the start to know the type of solo work on which you're interested in working. It may be that the material you are thinking about seems to require a specific presentational style, or it may be that you, as a performer, want to explore a particular form. Either way, you now need to determine if you have the necessary skills to create the work ahead of you.

If you're planning on doing *multiple character monologues,* do you feel capable of creating and playing a range of multiple characters, quite often in quick succession? If not, do you know where you can get the necessary help? You should be able to play characters of different ages and both sexes. You should also know how to comfortably do dialects. Also, being flexible and agile with your body is very helpful with multiple characters. If you need to take some classes in bodywork, I suggest starting prior to the rehearsal of your show.

For *autobiographical monologues,* you should be a good storyteller. Can you and are you willing to access (sometimes painful) memories from your past? Do you feel that your story will be of interest to an audience? Why? And ask yourself, why do you need to tell this story?

Your Sense of Truth

To be a good actor, you have to develop and rely on your own sense of truth in your work. That sense of truth is also a major asset in the creation of your own monologue material, no matter how long or short it is. It's the thing that will help you to honestly say what you want to say in the most personal way.

As an actor, I'm sure that you've had definite opinions and feelings about the material on which you've worked. Certain characters may have touched you more than others. Some moments, lines of dialogue, may have seemed more real to you. I'm not talking about judging a playwright's work; I'm talking about how you've responded to the material, from your personal sense of truth. *That sense of truth is like a divining rod in the work we'll be doing. Much of what this book is about is learning about your sense of truth, and how to access it and utilize it as a writer.*

4

Ways to Work, Selecting Your Tools

There are many tools that you can use to create your own material. They include writing it out with pad and pen, using a computer or typewriter, working with a tape recorder, working improvisationally, and working orally. Whichever way feels most comfortable to you and facilitates your work is the best way. I write and/or use the computer to create my monologues and books. But, for many years, I worked with pad and pen, and then on a word processor. How you work and what you choose to work with is as individual as who you are. You should experiment with several of the suggested ways to find out which works best for you.

Writing

This is the old pad and pen way of working. Many solo artists prefer this medium because of its tactile quality. There's a sense of your creative energy starting in your brain then going directly through your arm, to your hand, down into the pen, then onto the paper. It's quick, spontaneous, efficient. Many writers feel that this is the best way for them particularly during the exploratory stages, when they're just starting out on a new piece. As soon as an idea or some dialogue hits them they can immediately jot it down. Many artists are intimidated by machinery such as word processors and computers, and they find writing more actor-friendly.

Still, for many solo artists, the day begins with sitting in front of their computer, typing away in creative abandonment. Word processing programs such as Microsoft Word and Word Perfect enable you to shift phrases around, rearrange whole sections, catalogue what has been developed, and so on. There is no need to endlessly rewrite what has already been written, no carbon stained fingers, no pages lost or thrown out by mistake. It's an orderly, systematic, high-tech way to work.

The Internet can be a tremendous source of information for material that you're working on. By connecting with chat rooms you can have discussions with other writers and monologists who may be experiencing some of the same problems that you're trying to overcome. As well, today there are several monologue Web sites that you can connect to.

While we're talking about writing, it is important to mention that many solo performers carry a pad and pen with them at all times to take impulse notes (see the discussion of journal writing later on in this chapter). A great line of dialogue, an inspired moment for your monologue, or a keen insight should not be left to one's memory alone. You can be on a bus or walking down the street when you are struck with a great idea. It would be a shame to forget it. Just jot it down in your pad.

What Is Creative Writing?

Throughout much of this book, I'll be discussing writing in the creative sense of the word. At this point, I'd like to briefly discuss writing, not so much as an activity (paper and pad), but as an artistic process.

Writing is kind of like talking to yourself. Writers get to re-experience and even rethink moments of their lives. It is a way of understanding incidents and memories. By doing this you quite often get a new perspective, a new point of view of where you've been and what you've experienced. By revealing different parts of your life in your work, your audience may learn something about their own lives. *Writing is a form of communication, sharing, informing, and enlightening.*

HELPFUL BOOKS ABOUT CREATIVE WRITING

For those of you who would like to get some more information about the craft of writing, I recommend these books.

- *If You Want to Write* by Brenda Ueland (Graywolf Press)
  Like myself, Ms. Ueland believes that "everybody is talented, original, and has something important to say." This book is very inspiring, informative, and helpful, especially for those who feel a bit intimidated by the idea of writing.

- *Three Genres, the Writing of Poetry, Fiction, and Drama* by Stephen Minot (Prentice Hall, 6th Edition)
  This book explores the fundamental aspects of creative writing, including fiction writing, playwriting, and poetry.

Fear of Writing

There is always the fear that if you expose yourself in your writing, your audience will sit in judgment of you and your life. That fear is one of the great crosses all writers (and performers) have to bear. One of the secrets to quality writing is to not be too concerned about for whom you're writing. It should *always* be just for yourself. You can never second guess any audience, so why waste time worrying about the people for whom you're writing? If you honestly find that what you have to say is interesting or funny, it is more than likely that your audience will too. Jot it down.

Journal Writing

While working on your solo piece, you may want to keep a journal. Basically, a journal is like a diary. You put in it whatever interests you as you go through your day. Perhaps some of the material that you enter in the journal will be relevant and helpful to the piece that you're working on. Many monologists keep a journal with them at all times.

In the journal you will want to keep a record of such things as *your dreams.* Dreams are wonderful sources of subconscious information. Many artists rely heavily on their dreams for their creative work.

Observations are your day-to-day perceptions of the world around you and how you feel about things. The more descriptive you are about the things you see and feel, the more useful they might be later on.

Also, look at *your imaginary world.* We all have a fantasy life that pops in and out of our consciousness throughout the day. It can be very helpful to become aware of your fantasies on a conscious level. One way to use your imagination is to observe people and then imagine what their lives are like, where they're from, what they do for a living, and so forth.

You may find *photographs and ads* to be of use in your work. If you see an ad that interests you or triggers your imagination, paste it in your journal . If you come across a photo that brings up an old memory, paste it in your book

Looking at *paintings* can be very useful. Sometimes we respond to other artists' work and can be inspired by them. A painting of a man sitting in a bar can trigger a strong idea for a character monologue. A painting of a quiet street can remind you of the street you grew up on, which can bring up all kinds of memories that can be useful in your auto-biographical monologue.

Newspaper articles can also be of value in this type of work. Today's headlines can be terrific sources for new ideas and interesting stories. Many TV and film writers rely on the daily news as fodder for new material.

Using a Tape Recorder

Some monologists prefer not to type or write out their material. For them, the tape recorder is the most efficient way to work. They just turn it on and talk, more or less the same way that writers write and typists type. One bit of advice for those of you who plan on using a tape recorder: Make certain that all the tapes are very clearly marked. You should be able to locate any section of your recorded work. It's also been suggested that at some point you have someone type out the material from the tapes. You will need a script of some sort that can be used by the production teams at theaters in which you'll be performing.

Improvising: "Are You Talkin' to Me?"

Many actors enjoy the freedom of working totally improvisationally. If you've worked as an actor, you know that improvisation is a form of theater where no scripts are used. There are many different ways to approach and set up improvisational situations, from the highly structured to the completely free form. The really great thing about using your improvisational skills to create a monologue is that in improv, you give your mind permission to go wherever it wants and your mouth permission to say whatever comes out. When you improvise, you ignore the tiny censor in your head that sits in judgment, criticizing your every effort. The secret to successful improvisational work is to not put any restrictions on yourself, leaving yourself open to any impulse, physical or verbal. As you start working this way, you may want to tape-record your work. To some degree, much of the work we'll be doing on monologues incorporates some aspect of improvisation.

HELPFUL BOOKS TO LEARN ABOUT IMPROVISATIONAL WORK

- *Improvisation for the Theater* by Viola Spolin (Northwestern University Press)
  This is an essential book for those who want to learn improvisational work. Spolin works with theater games, which can also be a very useful way to develop material. She was one of the founders of modern improv.

- *Improv* by Keith Johnstone (Methuen)
  This is a wonderful book for those actors who are just starting out in improvisation. Johnstone explores the "nature of spontaneity," which is essential in the work we'll be doing.

- *Improv! A Handbook for the Actor* by Greg Atkins (Heinemann)
  This book, like the other two, focuses mainly on the theatrical application of improvisation in theater. Atkins has some wonderful improv exercises and offers some very interesting tidbits. This book is recommended for the beginner as well as those with some improvisation in their background.

Working Orally: In Front of an Audience

Some solo artists prefer to live their creative lives dangerously. They like to create their work on the edge of the sword. They develop their material improvisationally each night in front of a live audience. They "riff" (improvise) or ad-lib their dialogue in character (if they're doing character work), improvising completely from moment to moment. The dialogue that their character(s) speak changes nightly, a word here, a phrase there, sometimes even long sections are totally added or subtracted from the text. After each night's performance, the artist evaluates what he's done. Based on experience (and perhaps the director's feedback), the play changes, sometimes dramatically. It's not unusual for characters to be added or dropped, and entire sections to be totally reworked.

Spalding Gray says that he prefers to develop his autobiographical material in front of a live audience (see interview). The audience in the first preview of a new Spalding Gray show will see something quite different from the audiences that come later on. Some members of his audience come back several times to see how the work progresses. Generally, Gray starts out each show with just an outline of what he'll be talking about, and then let's the piece evolve night after night. How the material is received each night by the audience is a factor in how it changes. His original show may be up to an hour longer than the final ones. Even after it opens, Gray said that he continues working on the material, refining it, and reshaping it (but to a lesser degree) indefinitely.

Danny Hoch riffs his character monologues each night in front of his audience. Generally he says that he knows what his characters will be talking about, their themes and ideas. But as he works in front of the audience each night, like Spalding Gray, the work evolves. Also like Gray, he hones and develops material based on audience reaction. Hoch says that in his case, his director, Jo Bonney, (see Jo Bonney's interview) is also a major contributing factor to his rewriting process.

Working Orally: Developing Your Stories throughout the Day

Another way monologists develop their stories is by telling and retelling the same story to different people throughout the day. They repeat this process over a period of weeks or months. By constantly retelling the story, they hone it down, refine it, perfect it. They edit out unnecessary phrases or sections that they've noticed didn't work in prior tellings.

They bring the developed story to small audiences. They continue refining the piece first in workshops, then during previews, right until the show's opening.

Charlayne Woodard (see interview) mentioned that for up to a year before she creates one of her solo shows, she constantly tells different people the same story, "sometimes at dinner parties, sometimes to friends on the street." Usually her stories are anecdotal recollections of her childhood with her family. She watches listeners for their reactions to the story, especially noticing any emotional response. Ms. Woodard says that she'll tell the same story dozens of times before deciding whether or not she'll actually include it in her show.

5

PREPARING

In the beginning, there's just your will and determination. But for many actors, facing that blank sheet of paper or that empty cassette in the tape recorder can be intimidating. One thing to keep in mind when working on your own material is that the better prepared you are early on, the easier your work will be later.

For Those Actors Who Know Which Type (Style) of Monologue They Want to Create

If at this point you know the form that you want your short monologue or monologue play to take (e.g., character monologues, autobiographical narrative monologue, etc.), then look at the list below. This list can also be of use to those of you who have a specific story that you want to tell in your monologue.

The purpose of this outline is to jump-start your thinking about the piece that you'll be working on. It's just an eye opener, a preliminary look at future possibilities. We will be working on a detailed outline later on.

- Start out by listing any ideas that you now have regarding the piece. Put down whatever comes to mind, no matter how ridiculous it might seem to you. List your intentions, your goals, your dreams for the piece. Let yourself go as far as you can with this wish list.

- List any things that you feel you may need to research later on. If you're work-ing on character monologues, list any ideas that you have for potential charac-ter material (and anything that might connect these characters).
- This is a very early phase of your work. Don't be too concerned if things go in a very different direction as you actually begin working on the piece.

For Those Actors Who Don't Know What Type of Solo Material They Want to Create

Some actors start off on a project knowing that they want to do a solo show, but they don't know what form or even what subject they'd like to explore. For those of you in this category, perhaps the following material will be of help.

Spend some time exploring, researching, opening yourself up to new ideas that may be fodder for your monologue. Take as long as you need for this research, a few weeks, months, whatever. You might also want to reread the earlier section in this book on keeping a journal. Keep the following thoughts in mind during your search:

- There's no shortage of ideas; they're everywhere, all around us, all the time.
- Keep an ongoing list of all possibilities for your piece. Don't be stingy, put any-thing down that comes to mind, no matter how ridiculous it may seem.
- Become a people watcher. Go to parks and malls. Noticing how and what peo-ple are communicating to each other can tremendously inform your work, especially if you decide to develop character monologues. As you watch people, listen to what they're saying; notice what they're *not* saying. Be aware of their body language, their movement, their rhythms, even their wardrobe.
- Let your imagination run wild as you watch people. Ask yourself as many ques-tions about them as you can think of. Who are they? Are they married? What do they do for a living? What is their family life like? What do you think their secrets are?
- Other things that you can use to inform your work: music, theater, even TV. These may be things you've always been aware of, but now your perception, your intention, your focus, is different.
- Start to search your memory. Think about what your life has been like so far. The value of memories is invaluable in this kind of work. Some of your stories may be very funny, some embarrassing, and some very painful. Tennessee Williams, Arthur Miller, and many other great playwrights created some of their greatest works based on actual events from their childhoods. One thing that certainly makes you different from anyone else is your personal memory, your past experience.
- Try to imagine what your future will be like. Think about what you'll be doing in ten years, in twenty-five years, longer.

• Read works by other monologists. See what types of monologues personally interest you. If someone is performing a one-person show in your area, try to see it. Also, there are several one-person shows on videotape. Spalding Gray's *Swimming to Cambodia* and Julie Harris in *The Belle of Amherst* are just a couple.

Perking with an Idea

Perhaps you've had an idea for a piece and don't know yet how you want to express it. Sometimes it's better not to do anything for a while, just let it perk. Many artists talk about an initial gestation period before they do any actual work on a new piece. This is very different than using delay tactics to avoid work. By letting an idea perk, you're trusting that your subconscious mind will collect the necessary information for you. Like little elves in the night, the subconscious instinctively knows how to gather and organize the material you've been looking for.

Looking at your dreams and keeping a journal during this time may also be very helpful.

Deciding When to Begin

The right time to begin is obviously when you feel ready, when you know that you'll have the time to put into the work ahead of you. But perhaps out of fear, many writers procrastinate, putting off the starting date with one excuse after another. If writing your own monologue is really something that you want to do, then my advice is just do it, begin. It's amazing how things fall into place once you get the ball rolling.

Guidelines for Creating Short or Audition Monologues

Now that you have selected the tools you'd like to work with and have some preliminary ideas of what you think your piece will be about, let's discuss some of the technical aspects of monologue writing. As I mentioned earlier, the monologue form is a very flexible form, with flexible rules. However, since the short monologue and the audition monologue have more strictures, especially when it comes to time, I'd like to give you some of the basic rules. While rules are made to be broken, I offer these because I have found them to work.

There are several attributes that a good short monologue (audition monologue, character monologue) should include. It should generally be from two to eight minutes in length. Because of its brevity, your story shouldn't be too complex or convoluted. I don't advise spending too much time on exposition in a short monologue, it tends to drag the piece down and bore your audience. Although narrative short monologues do work, monologues that include strong, immediate dialogue and have an intense, passionate, and exciting story are generally much more effective, especially for auditions where you want to wow them.

Generally, a short monologue doesn't include too many characters. Having too many characters tends to confuse the listener. Also, it's difficult to develop multiple characters in a short amount of time.

The short monologue, actually all monologues, should have a clear *beginning, middle, and end.* I know that this seems obvious, but by being aware of it and adhering to it, you'll be able to avoid structural problems while developing your piece. I'm sure you've seen monologues that seem to hop all over the place, losing the audience along the way, or monologues that seem to just stop rather than end. These monologues are examples of pieces that need a strong beginning and end. Monologues that set out to handle a large issue and then suddenly end, without sufficiently dealing with that issue, generally need a stronger middle. Each one of these three portions of your monologue must be given its due. Your sensitivity to your own material is the guiding force that allows you to know when each section has sufficiently expressed what your character(s) needs to say. In most (but not all) monologues, the main character wants to achieve some goal. In the middle section we see him struggle to get what he wants. By the end of the monologue he'll either get it or he won't. Generally speaking, the middle section of your monologue will dominate because it deals with action and plot development.

Your monologue should include an objective, an obstacle, and an arc. Just to clarify, the character's *objective* is what he wants, what he feels he must have. (The action of a piece begins when we know what the character's *objective* is), an *obstacle* can be described as any obstruction, hindrance, or opposition that stands in the way of a character's getting something that he wants. The *arc* is the shape the monologue takes. It is the through-line from the beginning to the middle to the end. The arc is determined by the journey that the character takes to get what he wants or needs.

If you are writing a performance art piece you still need to have a beginning, middle, and end. You want your audience to be able to somehow follow the progression of the monologue, no matter how abstract or nonnarrative the piece is. Since you are not telling a story in the conventional sense, it is your job to create your own set of ground rules and structure and then to diligently maintain what you've set up. How you choose to express yourself (i.e., with dance, multimedia, music, etc.) is very much a part of the selection process of a performance artist. The canvas may be different than that of a conventional storyteller, but the challenge and demand to tell some sort of story, express some sort of message, is still the same.

Unlike a play, a monologue does not always have to have conflict in it. Strong characterization and dialogue are sometimes enough to keep the monologue interesting and theatrical. It should be able to answer the following questions:

1. **Where am I physically when I'm delivering this monologue?**
    Letting the audience know where you are (in the context of your story) is helpful in their understanding and sharing of what it is you're trying to tell. In the case of autobiographical monologues, you may be back in the house that you grew up in. If you can clearly establish this location for your audience, you set a mood and bring them into your world. In some monologues, you may be acting as your story's narrator. There may be no pretense that you are in a make-believe location. You are just in the theater, telling the story of your monologue to the audience. Often, during monodramas, there is little or no scenery. It is therefore your job as the storyteller to fill the stage with images that will somehow create the world that you're trying to evoke.

2.   **If I'm talking to someone in this piece, who is this person in my life?**

The secret to dealing with this aspect is not to bog your monologue down with a lot of facts about the person you're talking to. How you relate to them, what you're saying, and how you say it will give the audience most of the important information. Certainly some relevant facts about the relationship may be necessary. But by calling someone "mom" or "honey," you immediately give obvious clues about the relationship.

3.   **Why am I telling this story?**

This information is central to any monologue. The audience must get a sense of why you're standing there in front of them in the first place. This need to express yourself is central to the storytelling aspect of any good monologue. The need to tell this story cannot be general; it must be specific. Your character may need to rid himself of some pain from his past, or he may have this hilarious story that he must tell someone or he'll just burst. Or it may be some profound insight that that he feels must be shared with the rest of the world, now! Whatever you select, remember, the need to tell, the urgency, should be a propelling force. Think of a short monologue as a miniature one-act play.

If the monologue that you're working on is specifically for audition material, there are certain things to keep in mind. Many of the items listed below deal mainly with the marketing aspect of audition monologues, but since the purpose of an audition monologue is largely marketing, these are significant considerations.

You should create characters that you know you're capable of playing and that are within your grasp as a writer. Take into consideration the pressure you'll be under while auditioning. *This is not a time to emotionally stretch. Work on characters that show off your best assets as an actor.* If you're not good at physical comedy or gut wrenching emotions, don't create characters with whom you will need to portray these things.

While it may seem like overkill to repeat this, it is particularly important that an audition monologue have a clearly defined beginning, middle, and end. In a bare rehearsal hall with no lights or costumes to help you, you will only have your words, your body, and your voice to indicate to the viewers when you've started performing, when you've reached the high point, and when the piece is finished. You want to indicate to the auditioners that you are professional enough to accomplish this, in a tight time slot, and with no technical support.

Remember, auditioners who often see dozens of actors usually make these decisions quickly. You don't want to be cut off before you show your stuff. Try to keep the monologues down to about two minutes in length (less is more).

You should develop an assortment of monologues, each of which will be appropriate for different audition situations. *As part of your repertoire, you should have a comedic monologue, a dramatic one, and if you feel so inclined, a surreal or stylized one.*

FUNDAMENTALS OF
ALL GOOD MONOLOGUES

I'm listing these particular attributes here because I believe that most good monologues contain them. Before you build the bridge I think it's always a good idea to know where it's going to go. But don't think that these are absolute or unbreakable. *The only rules that you must follow for your monologue writing are the ones that you create, that work for you.*

Good monologue plays, no matter what form they take, should have a well-defined structure, just as a good play would. Even a performance art piece, which doesn't follow some of the basic rules of form, should have its own truthful structure.

In his monologue play *St. Nicholas,* Conor McPhearson has his character recall a chilling story of a particular night of drinking when he encountered a vampire. The story takes a narrative form. Occasionally, the man will reenact a moment with present tense dialogue. The story has a very defined clear beginning, middle, and end. It builds in tension as we experience what our main character tells us about this very scary night. In some ways this is similar to a bizarre bedtime story. We, the audience, go along with our storyteller as he takes us from one moment to the next in a "and then, . . . " kind of suspense, discovering what happened next along the way. The structure (and arc) of this suspense-filled monologue is as old as storytelling itself.

In his play *Mambo Mouth,* John Leguizamo creates a series of character monologues. Each of the individual monologues in his play features family members and friends from his past. Each tells its own individual story, with a beginning, middle, and end. The form of these monologues, by and large, is dialogue-based, with the character talking directly to the audience, conversationally. It is through the culmination of all of these individual monologues that the audience sees a larger story and gets an understanding of what it was like being "a Latin from Manhattan."

You can see that these two examples, *Mambo Mouth* and *St. Nicolas*, employ very different styles and structures to tell a story to an audience. There is no one rule as to how a monologue must be structured. *The story should always dictate the form.*

Like the short monologue, monologue plays should have a clear beginning, middle, and end. Remember: No matter what form it takes, your monologue play is a way of telling a story, and all good stories have a clear through-line.

The story that you're telling should be able to sustain interest for however long it takes to tell. This doesn't mean that you need to concern yourself solely with the entertainment value of the play. But keep in mind that there is an audience out there. *Make sure that the story you're performing is theatrical and not something that the audience could have stayed home and read. Always remember, you're writing for the theater.*

Your play, like the short monologues discussed in the previous chapter, should usually include an objective, an obstacle, and an arc. Like the short monologue, the monologue play doesn't always have to have a strong conflict for it to work theatrically, but having one can certainly be advantageous.

You may create as many characters as you want, just be sure that each one of them is necessary to your story; you don't want to overpopulate the piece. Each character should be fully developed and different from the others.

You may have as many scenes and settings as you wish, but just be sure that the audience always knows where they are in your play.

At some point, your audience should become aware of your point of view, of what you're trying to say. I hate to say "message" because that conjures up some sort of didactic sermon. But for any play to succeed, the audience should have some sense of why the writer took the time to create it in the first place. If you'll recall, I mentioned earlier that one of the main reasons to create your own monologue should come out of a need to express something that deeply concerns you. It may be a burning issue or some event(s) in your past that you need to personally resolve. The important thing is that during your monologue you attempt to come to grips with the issue or the meaning of the events. You don't have to resolve it, but you do need to at least show us why you've decided to discuss it in the first place.

John Leguizamo has said that one the of the main reasons that he wrote *Mambo Mouth* and *Spic-O-Rama* was so that he could better understand more about his family and the neighborhood he grew up in, and to be able to share this with others.

Evan Handler wrote *Time on Fire* to reveal how we can become victims of medical bureaucracy when dealing with doctors and hospitals when we are seriously ill. In both Leguizamo's and Handler's cases the writing of their material was cathartic for them, as well as entertaining and educational for their audiences.

I feel I must once again mention that the most important thing to keep in mind is that all monologues and monologue plays must have *an interesting story to tell, a good yarn, a reason for us in the audience to want to be there in the first place.*

To Whom Is the Character Speaking?

This is a very important question to answer when working on a monologue. Many actors, when asked, "Why is your character speaking?" will often answer, "Because he feels like it," or simply, "He needs to." When asked, "Who is the character speaking to?" Many actors are uncertain, and answer something like, "I guess to anyone." It is the monologue writer's job, at the very least, to provide some clues that will assist the actor in answering these questions.

One way of dealing with this is by imagining to whom your character is speaking. Is it to the actual audience in front of him? Is it to a specific character referred to in the monologue? Or is the character speaking "into the abyss?"

You must invent a dynamic character who absolutely must speak, must reveal his inner self. The character must have a powerful need to express his thoughts: That is why he is speaking.

In theater, as in real life, the words that people (or characters) say are influenced by the people to whom they are speaking. As an actor, you have surely discovered that what you are trying to get and from whom you are trying to get it influence your choice of actions. As a writer, you must create a character with strong, specific needs and desires. This is especially true in character driven and narrative pieces.

Sometimes monologists place imaginary characters on the stage so that the character has someone with whom to speak. One thing I strongly advise against is having these imaginary characters speak back to your main character. It forces the main character to take pauses to listen and then, quite often, waste valuable stage time repeating the questions just asked by the imaginary character. That device can become tiresome very quickly.

Questions Every Monologue Must Answer

Since monologues are stories, they must be held accountable for the basic ingredients that are true of any story. Answering the following questions in your monologue will give it detail, depth, and texture. Also, the more information you, the writer, have about what you're creating, the richer your work can be. I'm not suggesting writing information out in some factual way but, rather, being able to creatively reveal important information to your audience within the dialogue or narrative. I'm sure that as an actor, you were constantly trying to learn as much information as you could about the character you were playing. The same holds true here.

Who?

This refers to the character. Who is he or she? You must know your character inside out. You should be able to improvise in that character if necessary. You should be able to imagine the character in situations other than the one you are presenting in your piece.

What?

What problems or complications arise for this character? To make something dramatic there should be some sort of conflict, something that stirs the character into action.

When?

Are we in the present, or are we in the past or the future? What is the time of day? Is it 4 A.M. or three in the afternoon? Obviously, these facts will affect how characters speak, move, and think.

Where?

What is the setting? Are we dealing with a character or characters who live on Park Avenue, or is he a beggar on the street? Your audience must get a sense (preferably early on in your piece) of where they are. How does this location affect the character who is speaking?

Why?

Through the character's dialogue, let us know why the character is saying and doing the things he is. The audience must have some sense of what motivates the character; otherwise, they will become confused and eventually disinterested.

How?

How does your character resolve the complication that you've set up? The way he goes about solving his dilemma or conflict is one of the main components of storytelling. Specifically how a character resolves his problem is often an indication of whether we are watching a comedy or drama.

About Autobiographical Monologues

Unlike fictional monologues, autobiographical ones require a somewhat different preparation. Since your life is the main source for the material, you'll need to access pertinent information from your past. Reviewing parts or all of your life for material will not only be informative to you, but can also be a source of inspiration and illumination to your audience. Sometimes the things that we consider to be the most private are in fact quite universal and can be understood by everyone in the audience.

IF YOU NEED TO JUMP-START YOUR MEMORY FOR MATERIAL

- Look through desks, drawers, and closets for any photos, letters, old diaries, old toys, or any other source of memorabilia that may trigger some recollections.
- Try to recall, in as much detail as you can, *that first romance you had that you thought you'd never get over.* What was it about that person that excited you? How do you feel about the experience now?
- Many people have a *turning point* in their life. Did you? Think about what your life was like before that event? How did it change afterward?
- Think about *an important job* you once had. What was important about it? How did it change you?

- Recall, as painful as it might be, *the death of someone you really cared about.* How did that affect you then? How does it affect you now?
- Think about a *relative, friend, or teacher who somehow influenced you,* changed your life in some dramatic way. What was so special about this person? How did he or she influence your life?
- Thinking about *past holidays* usually brings up memories. Was there a particular holiday that will always bring strong memories? What happened?
- There may have been a *dream that you had growing up,* something that you really wanted to do, but never got to (or perhaps did). How did that affect your life?
- At any point in your life, *have you or someone that you loved been ill with some life threatening or incapacitating disease?* What was the story surrounding that period?

As you can see, these suggestions are just memory triggers. If your monologue is about a specific period of your life, try to recall, in as much detail as you can, what was going on both internally and in the world around you. Recalling world events creates a context for your story.

Another thing to keep in mind is a list of the characters that you're going to include from that period of your life. Recalling the exact things that they said is the ideal, but unfortunately we usually can't. But we can recall things like what they wore. If you think back, a particular day or moment may come to mind. Notice specifically what people were wearing. Try to remember every detail of their wardrobe. How their hair looked. Were they carrying a purse? Were they wearing earrings? What was their make-up like? Can you recall the smell of their cologne? Do you remember any specific mannerisms that they had? The way they held their head when listening to you? A look in their eyes when they ate something they liked? Their look of disapproval when they saw someone they didn't like? Try to remember any idiosyncratic things they did.

Try to remember how you felt about them back then. Have your feelings toward them changed? It's interesting how after people are gone, our feelings toward them change, sometimes dramatically. That change in feelings can be very helpful when writing about them.

Interviewing relatives and family friends can be a useful source for gathering information that you may not recall. Return, if you can, to the old neighborhoods that you grew up in. Walk around, look at familiar buildings and streets, see what it conjures up. See if people you knew still live there. Perhaps pay a visit. Interview them if it feels comfortable and is practical to do so.

Storytelling Monologues

Actor Scott Robertson took the storytelling workshop lead by Spalding Gray (see Gray's interview) at The Esalen Institute in Big Sur. Robertson recalls, "There were eight participants in the workshop. Their assignment was to 'tell a story that could engage the rest of the group.' They'd meet three times a day for eight days to tell their stories."

According to Scott, "Spalding believes that we all have a story in us. That story can be something that once happened to us, an event, something that changed our life. Or it may be our life story, what's happened to us along the way to make us become who we are today.

"The participants were assigned to tell their story in thirty minutes and then tell their story again in ten minutes. The purpose was for clarity, to eliminate extraneous information."

One thing Scott said he learned from his experience was that images are one of the main things that capture an audience. The more specific and descriptive you can be, the better. How you feel/felt about the event of the story that you're telling is another important thing to keep in mind. Storytelling is about saying something out loud to people who are listening. Words, images, and ideas are what we communicate to make our stories alive, vibrant, and interesting.

Narrative and Dramatic Style

I think it's important to describe the difference between narrative and dramatic writing, since both styles are interwoven throughout most monologues.

In the narrative style, a narrator (sometimes in character) *tells* a story. There is a great deal of background material with very detailed descriptions. Character, setting, and plot are developed in these detailed descriptions. Generally speaking, autobiographical monologues use more of the narrative style than other types of monologues.

In the dramatic style, *we're shown, in strong dramatic actions, rather than told the story.* Quite often the monologist has the character start out directly into the middle of an action. For instance, the character may start the monologue ranting about some issue, or appealing to the audience for something. The story is happening right there in the moment, before our eyes. While in this case there is no need to go through the beginning, middle, and end of the *narrative,* the piece itself still needs to have an *arc* to it.

Your Personal Style: Your Voice

Your "voice" is your style, your way of expressing yourself. Your voice stems directly from your sense of truth, which we spoke of earlier. It is your unique choice of words and phrases, your rhythm, the way you speak, your vision, how you tell your story. It is your trademark style. It is a major factor in determining the tone of your work. All good writers, successful monologists, and performance artists have their own distinct voice. Finding and developing your personal voice is an integral part of your work as a monologist. The trap for most beginning monologists is to try to emulate (whether consciously or unconsciously) their favorite writer's style. To avoid this happening, always stay focused on specifically what it is you want to say, on your need to tell your story, and on creating your characters exactly the way you see and feel them.

When Working Specifically on Character Monologues

First, let your imagination take you inside the character's head as you see it. Stay there a while, breathe it in, live in his shoes. Imagine what it's really like to be him. Notice the differences/similarities between who you are and who he is. Notice how he thinks and feels about things. When you feel that you really know the character, viscerally, let the character speak. Improvise different scenarios.

I was working on a character that I called Lila for my book *Street Talk*. Lila danced on *Hullabaloo*, a 1960s TV show, and went on to become a sleazy go-go dancer. I'm not a woman, I never danced on *Hullabaloo*, and I was never a sleazy go-go dancer. When I started working on her, I recalled watching that TV show. I recalled thinking about what it must be like to have millions of Americans watching you dance on TV. I allowed myself to imagine a whole different world than my own. I allowed myself to feel what it might be like go-go dancing in a bar. As funny as it might seem, I danced around my apartment, pretending I was in a go-go cage. I tried to imagine what the bar must be like with men, many of them drunk, looking up at me, desiring me. The more I imagined Lila's world, the clearer the character became, and the easier it was to speak her voice. The trap is to speak "in character" prematurely, to come from your head the way you think the character would speak. What happens then is that you create characters that are stereotypes, ungrounded, and ultimately difficult to perform.

Once you have found the character, letting him speak improvisationally, you'll find his story, what it is he has to say. Many playwrights mention that they really don't write their plays; rather, they say that the plays write themselves. Let your character lead you where he wants to go. Let your character tell the story that he wants to tell. Just get out of the way; just "play."

Always try to simplify things; bring them down to their basic truth. You can always elaborate later in rewrites. *There is nothing more boring on stage than long-winded, unnecessary narratives that could easily be stated in a line or two of dialogue.* Use the facts of what you're trying to say as a guideline for how you'll say it. Review the "Questions Every Monologue Must Answer" section of this chapter.

Even if there is a surreal, poetic, or stylized quality to the monologue that you're working on, initially try to say the lines as you would say them in your everyday life. As you become more comfortable in your monologue's style, you'll find that you're able to speak the "new language" freely, more appropriately to the style.

Once again, keep in mind that you are writing for the stage, not for a book. You don't want to become too literary, too cerebral; your audience will fall asleep on you.

To sum it all up:

• Write as you think
• Write as you feel
• Write as you speak

Examples of Different Voices and Styles

As I mentioned earlier, one of the main goals of this book is to help you find your own voice as a monologist. To give you some idea of how diversified this field is, I've reprinted some excerpts from some well-known monologists. Notice the differences in their styles. Notice their choice of words, phrases, and ideas.

From *An Evening with Quentin Crisp* by Quentin Crisp

I've been told that I equate wealth with style. I don't, but I would say this: To a physicist, money would be the solid state of style. There's no other connection between the two. And of this, also, I can give you an example.

Until recently there was in Soho, the hooligan district of London, a woman known as "The Countess." But in spite of her imperial style, she had in fact no fixed address, no means of support, and her body was perpetually bent double from a lifelong habit of looking in the trashcans to see if she could possibly find something there she could sell to a kind friend—or, if not, that she herself could use. And one day, in a trashcan in the most expensive part of London, she found a complete backless bead dress. She longed for night to fall, so that she could nip into a dark doorway and try it on. But by about half-past six, her patience had worn out. It was barely twilight, but she went into a churchyard in the middle of London and there she proceeded to take her clothes off. This caused a crowd to collect—and the crowd caused the policemen to collect. And the next day, in court, when the magistrate said, "And what exactly were you doing stripping among the dead?" she replied, "I was doing what any woman would be doing at that hour—changing for dinner."

So you see, however grandiose the style you may have chosen for yourself, you will not need any actual money to support it—and more than that, you won't even need talent.

Quentin Crisp generally writes in a light, witty tone. There is a sense of polite, gentle humor in his work. His style has a relaxed eloquence. Much of what he writes is a commentary on social behavior (including his own). He tells his sometimes-autobiographical stories in a narrative, anecdotal style, rarely acting out any of the characters. Mr. Crisp generally remains seated during his shows and talks directly to his audience as if they were visiting him in his parlor.

Winfred from *Monster* by Dael Orlandersmith

I'm thinkin' of my girl Theresa. An I'm feelin' bad 'cause, you know, she ain't with me, right? I mean, you know what I'm talkin' about? Like when

your woman ain't around, man. Dat's some hard shit. (beat) She write poet-
ry and listen to classical and rock. You know 'bout that shit, right? Well my
girl, she like it too. (beat) You should see her, man, she got soft smooth skin.
Yeah, an she got much booty—I likes dat booty, man. In order for me to
peep a broad she got to have some ass. Gots to. (beat) Man, ever since we
wuz kids she wuz writin' poetry and stuff to me, thru the wall. Readin' thru
da wall. See, the buildin' I lived in, right, her mother owned. Me, my sister
Marsha and my mother live there. And me, Theresa an Marsha wuz friends.
Tight, like family, right? Like I would look after dem, you know, 'cause it's
rough. (beat) Like I protect Theresa. Nigga's round the way hated her 'cause
she listened to rock and all that shit, and dressed different from them. But
see, dey ain't know her like I did. Nigga's wanted to get next to her, man—
see, dat's what it wuz. And they wuz jelous, 'specially when I tole 'em how
she would talk to me though the wall.

Dael Orlandersmith creates character monologues that reflect her experience as a black woman growing up in Harlem. Her language is rough and poetic. She's been called "a poetic sybarite, a black female Walt Whitman drunk with the power to pummel." Her choice of words and phrases reflect the neighborhood where she grew up. Her characters express the darker side of life. She does not attempt to make things nice. Her characters are blunt, raw. Yet there is a yearning, a need within all of her characters to be heard, to express themselves.

John W. from *Two Minute Monologs* by Glenn Alterman

Sittin' here by the window with my old cat, Carl; lookin' out at the snow
fallin', drinkin' my coffee, tryin' to decide what to do today. Should I go out,
should I stay in? Carl doesn't seem to have too much of an opinion on it
though. So I just talk to him about the snow. Tell him how cold it is out there
today, how lucky he is to be inside here where it's warm. Carl just purrs and
listens and looks out at the snow through half opened eyes. He's a damn
good listener, Carl. Should give a course in it to some of the people in the
town here, I'll tell ya. Purrs so loud you'd think I was talking to him about
a warm sunny day in Florida rather than the mess we got here in Maine
today. He appreciates, Carl, he does. Remembers that rainy night when I
found him downtown all cut up, bleeding and thin and took him home here
and nursed him, stood vigil, and saved all his nine lives in that one night.
Carl remembers, I'm sure. I'm sure he does. He'll put his paw across my
sockless foot and lean his head there, looking up at me as I talk about
whatever, forever, doesn't matter. He's got no opinions on any of it. Then
pretty soon his eyes start to close letting me know that he's about to fall

asleep and dream . . . Oh I don't know, whatever the hell cats dream about.
Then one last wink letting me know that my words and voice are a happy
place for him. (Smiling) He's my best friend. Then he's asleep, as I contin-
ue petting him, looking out at the town from my window seat. Watching
the snow fall, drinking my coffee, trying to decide what the hell I'm going
to do today.

John W. is a character monologue. The character is somewhat passive, lonely, indeci-
sive. John is a procrastinator whose life is passing him by. He seems to hope that his
cat will somehow help him make a decision, which of course it can't. Notice John's
words and thoughts. Notice what he says about the people in the town in which he
lives. When he talks about Carl, his cat, he says, "He (Carl) should give a course in it
(listening) to some of the people in the town here." You assume that many people in
the town probably don't listen to what John has to say; perhaps they even ignore him.
Part of the secret to understanding his character is to understand the relationship
with his cat. By saying "he appreciates, Carl, he does," we learn that John W., too,
appreciates, (having Carl).

From *An Evening with Shelly Mars* by Shelly Mars

I had a big strong jock dad. I was his girl-boy. His tomboy. I was like his
girlfriend boy. I remember going by the drive-in and I said, "Dad, let's go to
the drive-in and watch a movie." We always loved to sneak in places, get in
free, being Jews and all. So he turned off the headlights, and we snuck
through the exit. We were hanging out, and I remember a porno preview
flashed on screen. It was a big blonde babe getting banged from behind, by
a black midget, and blondee kept screaming, "You're the best baby Daddy,
baby Daddy, you're the best!" I was 10 years old. Two years before Hermes.
It was exciting. I remember turning into a boy (Shelly acts this out.) My dad
turned to me and said, "Ah, don't look!" I answered in a really deep voice,
"Yeah, whatever."

Shelly Mars has been described as a self-styled transgender expert and drag king. Her
writing is a combination of satire, reverence, and humor. Her stories are part autobiographical, part fantasy, and part sexual odyssey. She digs into her various closets and
shares uncensored and provocative commentary on herself and the world around her.
Her writing has a feeling of "I've-been-around-the-block-baby" and is filled with street
savvy and wisdom. You can also notice a humorous self deprecating tone to her work.
When referring to the drive-in, she says, "We always loved to sneak in places, get in free,
being Jews and all." Shelly doesn't care about political correctness. Her humor is meant
to constantly push the envelope.

From *Gray's Anatomy* by Spalding Gray

Ron was marrying us. He had joined the Universal Church of God in Fresno, California, for thirty-five dollars. We had written the ceremony together, and he spoke it beautifully, ending with, "May this couple be together for as long as they both shall love."

> *We run down to the sea together to look out, and then we went back to the house to celebrate.*
>
> *I drink vodka and I drank white wine and I ate big fish.*
>
> *I ate steamed vegetables and I ate wedding cake. I drank coffee and I smoked a cigar. I drank brandy.*
>
> *And I ate and I drank and I smoked . . . everything that could make me blind.*
>
> *Thank you for coming.*

Spalding Gray writes autobiographically. He tells his highly personal stories in what he calls his "neurotic, ironic, nonathletic voice." His monologues are a way for him to confront his personal demons of neurosis, immaturity, and mistrust. You get the impression that he is sitting directly across from you at a table talking, which indeed is what he does when he performs his shows.

Gray is a storyteller, and views about his life are the stories that he tells. He doesn't attempt to act out his characters, but lets you know them in his very descriptive storytelling. He uses strong images and descriptive narrative phrases. His stories work on multiple levels, with seemingly unrelated stories coming together as a whole. Notice particularly, his use of tense, past and present (within the same sentence). It reveals how he sees that particular moment in his mind.

Sam from *Jails, Hospitals and Hip-Hop* by Danny Hoch

(A corrections officer in his early thirties sits in the waiting room of an upstate New York psychologist.)

Hi, hello. How are you? . . . Who are you? Oh, you're Doctor Lemmings? Yeah, Hi hello. Sam Knoll. Oh, I thought you were the secretary? Oh, that's cheap. I mean, that's smart, save money, I don't want to get into a whole thing. So you're the doctor? Great. . . . No, I mean, women doctors, they exist, I don't wanna, ya know . . . go there. . . . Oh, you're not finished? You're still with a patient? Well I mean . . . I'm here! On time. I want you to mark down that I arrived for the session on time, because I went out of my way to be on time. . . . No, that's alright. I mean, what am I gonna do? You gotta do what you gotta do, I'll . . . I'll make a phone call. . . . No, that's all right. I got my own, thanks.

Danny Hoch writes character monologues. He has the rare ability to represent people as they really are. He gets inside of his characters' heads and shows their souls with compassion and humor. Many of his characters are angry, streetwise misfits. The dialogue in this piece is conversational, urban. This monologue concerns a corrections officer who is under psychiatric evaluation for roughing up a prisoner but is most worried about his child visitation rights following his broken marriage. Notice Hoch's use of dialogue. Notice the dialogue he uses to reveal things about this particular character. Lines like "Hi hello. Sam Knoll." The dialogue is succinct, with no wasted words. Or, "I mean, what am I gonna do? You gotta do what you gotta do." You can sense the type of person who's speaking by the way that he speaks, his exact choice of words.

From *Time on Fire* by Evan Handler

One month after Dr. Nixon's diagnosis, I came walking down the hallway of Sloan Kettering's twelfth floor. Earlier that day some bone marrow had been taken from the back of my hip to be examined and checked for any leukemia. If the marrow was clean, then I could go home, take a month off, before moving on to rounds two and three, known as "Consolidation Chemo."

In the room when I got there was Dr. Klaus and my parents. I tried my best to mask my awareness of what I was asking, and I faced Dr. Klaus and said, "Good news?"

"Yeah. Pretty good."

"What do you mean 'Pretty good'? Is it in remission or what?"

"Yeah, yeah, I'd say we have a very young, new, remission marrow. Don't get your hopes up too high, though. Still a long way to go." Then he added, "You know, that was one of the easiest inductions I've ever seen here."

I couldn't tell if he was congratulating me on a job well done, or telling me, "You just wait. We're gonna get you next time around."

Evan Handler's autobiographical monologue is a brutally frank and blisteringly angry account of his experience of having cancer and dealing with the medical establishment that treated him.

Mr. Handler has a novelist's eye for detail. Although he mainly writes in the narrative form, he pops in and out of present tense dialogue, reenacting short scenes, and then immediately returns to the narrative (which is the main form for his text). His use of the short scene vignettes gives the piece an "in the moment" reality.

One thing that is just touched on in this short selection is Handler's sense of humor. His use of humor makes this harrowing tale of cancer and hospital bureaucracy a very real and life-affirming story.

From *Oh My Goddess* by Sherry Glaser

She said, "Hello my name is reality and I will be your psychic tonight."

She said, "Tell me your name and birthday, and where you were born."

"Miguel De Cervantes, April 26th, 1965, San Diego."

She said, "Miguel, you are a powerful spirit."

I said, "That's right, you know it Mommy."

"Yes," she said, "You are destined for great things, but you are stuck on the Karmic wheel."

"It is as if you are always waiting for something."

I said, "Hey, I'm a waiter."

She said, "You see?"

She said, "I'm getting that you have been a waiter in every one of your past lives."

"No."

"In fact you were a waiter at the Last Supper. You must go back and confront your past."

"Go back?"

"Yes, you are having a special trance today, for only $42.95. I'll put you in a trance and take you back."

I said, "How are you going to put me in a trance over the phone?"

She said, "Do you have a speaker phone?"

"Yes."

"Just close your eyes and listen to the tones."

And she played a tune (he mimics the tune).

And I felt myself getting sleepier and sleepier and falling deeper and deeper into a trance.

When I opened my eyes I was standing in a little Italian place called Tony's on The Sea Of Galilee. Man, I'm telling you I was there, like I'm standing before you now.

I could smell the olive oil and the lemon from my cleaning rag.

And I could see the sea, the beautiful Sea of Galilee.

I'm cleaning up the tables after lunch, so actually, it was the last lunch, not the Last Supper, and up walks these thirteen guys.

And I'm thinking, "No way."

I said, "Hey, we're closed."

But then it's Jesus, Son of God. What a pain.

He never has any money, but . . .

I see he's with Judas.

Now I know a lot of bad things have been said about Judas Iscariot, but I'll tell you something about Judas, that guy was a good tipper.

Sherry Glaser's piece has a humorous, spiritual perspective. Her goal, she said, was to smash religious icons. In this play she is looking into religious myths and adding surreal humor. Miss Glaser says that she "wanted to bring a three dimensional aspect to religious beliefs, to bring them down to earth." She felt that the best way to do this was through humor. So she presents her character, Miguel, as any everyday guy going back to the Last Supper. His point of view is contemporary, practical, and unaffected. Much of his humor comes out of the comments that he makes about what he sees. For instance, being a waiter, seeing Jesus enter, and realizing that he probably has no money, he says, "What a pain"—hardly the comment one would expect about such a great religious leader.

From *Comedy That You Can Dance To* by Kate Clinton

So I've been living in New York, which is a fine thing, except that my big concern is that the Ed McMahon's Publishers Clearing House people would not be able to find our house. I didn't know if they went to apartments.

This was an interesting thing I found out in couple's therapy. I'm now going to couple's therapy, with my partner of course, because it would be silly otherwise. It's interesting because I'm now doing everything that I've always made fun of in my routines—except for guys of course.

Our therapist is wonderful. She's a brilliant therapist, but the big problem is, and I'm not complaining, she has a wandering eye. One eye goes off to the side. Now that is just not good in couple's therapy. We never know who she's really talking to. Our biggest fights are after therapy, when we say, "Oh well, when she said that nice thing she was looking right at me." I have actually found myself in therapy, leaning way to the left trying to get in her sight line. I found out in therapy, my partner actually fills out the map to our house so that Ed McMahon and the prize mobile could better find us on the great prize rewarding day. I was shocked because she believes that statistically, at some point, Ed McMahon has to go to a gay household. Unless they're presorting by zip codes. You know, West Hollywood, no way! Provincetown, good bye! I would love to see them open the door sometime on some square bottom dyke, wouldn't you? Or open the door on some fabulous queen who's just "Blaaaaah!!! Oh God, we can redecorate!"

Kate Clinton writes about life in the gay and lesbian scene as well as poking fun at the rest of society as she sees it. There is a sunny subversiveness to her material. Much of it is personal, anecdotal, and includes one-liners and even some jokes. She writes in a seemingly free-associating style, using language with an admirable precision.

From *Full Gallop* by Mary Louise Wilson and Mark Hampton

(SHE CROSSES TO PHONE, CAREFULLY PICKS UP RECEIVER AND LISTENS. THEN:)

Francoise!—I'll take this, Yvonne . . . Comment ca va . . . Je suis arrive!

Early this morning . . . Oh it was glorious. Just glorious. London, Milano, Madrid, Paris . . . No trouble with customs, no, but I did have a bit of a set—to getting off the plane . . . Well the stewardess attacked me with a Kleenex. "Here dearie, you've gone and got lipstick all over your ears!" Very efficient, these little steward . . . Oh, I'm tip-top! . . . Mmmm Really . . . I know, but I'm over it . . . It was ghastly. But I moved on . . . (SHE DISCOVERS A PACK OF LUCKIES BEHIND THE CUSHION WITH TWO CIGARETTES IN IT.)

Listen, you got my message? You're coming to dinner tonight? I realize it's short notice, but Va-Va Adlerberg will be here, and I've got a rather important party coming . . . Nubar Gulbenkian. You remember him? Always wore a green orchid in his lapel. . . . Awful, yes . . . I'll tell you all about it when I see you, but right now I have to ring off. I have to keep the line clear. I'm expecting his call. . . . The New York Post . . . about me? . . . Really . . . Well I'm not terribly curious. Why, is it vile? . . . Well, I won't. I never read that rag. . . . Around eight. Yup. Can't wait to see you! (SHE HANGS UP, GOES TO INTERCOM.) Demeyer! Baron Demeyer. That was the photographer I couldn't think of. Yvonne?

V.O.

(Oui)

Where did you put that copy of The New York Post?

V.O.

(Les Cigarettes)

Oh, the cigarettes, right. Now listen, the flowers have arrived, and . . . have you got ten dollars on you? (THERE IS A TINY PAUSE.)

V.O.

(Oui)

Give it to Lorenzo, he gave ten to the boy. (SILENCE.) And I'll reimburse you later. (SILENCE.) Merci.

There's no such thing as a slack French farce. Have you ever noticed this? I've given this a lot of thought, and I think it's because the French have to exercise their jaws so much and the insides of their mouth just to get the words OUT. Say "Bonjour" and see what your face does. (HOPEFULLY, THE AUDIENCE DOES.) Now. Try "Hi."

The best thing about my life in London was Paris. I adored Paris. I adore it! I adore it! I was born in Paris. Did I tell you that? And you don't get born in Paris to forget about clothes for five minutes. I was always going there for my clothes. I was MAD about clothes, and makeup and everything.

In the case of *Full Gallop*, the actress Mary Louise Wilson collaborated with writer Mark Hampton on a one-character play based on a previously published book, *D.V.*, about the life of fashion legend Diana Vreeland.

Ms. Wilson and Mr. Hampton worked on this play for several years, workshopping it all over the country before bringing it to New York and later London (where it received rave reviews).

Diana Vreeland was a formidable force in the fashion world from the 1940s until the 1970s. Ms. Wilson's Vreeland speaks to the audience as if they were guests in her living room. What she and Mr. Hampton have caught in their dialogue (and in the play) is the essence of Diana Vreeland.

Using Your Acting Technique to Create Character Monologues

Since this book is a book for actors who wish to write their own material, I feel that it's necessary to explore certain acting approaches that can assist you. Generally, actors are trained to work internally, that is, from the inside out, or externally, from the outside in. Either, or both of these approaches combined, can be helpful in developing fully realized characters for your monologues.

Working from the Outside in, as an Actor and Writer

Many actors, especially those who have studied the British technique for character development, work externally at first. Actors are informed about their characters from such external attributes as his/her age, speech mannerisms, appearance, and physicality. Actors gather information on these things from the dialogue in the play, the stage directions, and the action.

A Character's Age

A character's age quite often determines what he will think, feel, and do. It affects his behavior to some extent, perhaps how he'll be saying the monologue, and his dialogue.

The way the character views the world, his perceptions, are also based on his experiences in life. Younger characters will usually react differently to situations than older ones.

A CHARACTER'S VOCAL MANNERISMS

A character's vocal mannerisms can be very revealing. A character who has a speech impediment, or who speaks excessively slow or fast, or who hesitates while speaking tells us quite a bit about who they are by the way they talk. Many of these vocal mannerisms can be indicated in your stage directions.

BODY LANGUAGE

A character's body language begins with the way the character holds himself. Look around and you'll notice how people in the real world walk and move. Their physicality tells you a great deal about them. If they walk stoop-shouldered, head down, eyes to the floor, it's a reliable indication of something about their personality. If someone holds his head high, chest out, looks straight ahead, with a warm smile on his face, that tells us something else about him, doesn't it? A character's physical attributes can be a great aid in helping to trigger the imagination. It's a useful tool that you shouldn't overlook in developing your character monologues.

THE CHARACTER'S APPEARANCE

A character's appearance tells us a great deal about him. A homeless person certainly looks different than a member of royalty. Does your character seem proud of the way he looks? Is he unkempt, a slob? Is he out of touch with how he looks? How does the way the character looks affect his behavior? Your character's outer appearance can be handled in your stage directions. Quite often in an evening of character monologues, the actor and director will choose not to change wardrobe during the play because of time restrictions. Sometimes something as simple as a hat, a scarf, or a jacket can suggest all that is needed. Eric Bogosian and Danny Hoch (see interview) dress in black pants and black tee shirt and don't change costumes during their shows. We learn about their characters by the way they move, their physicality, how they speak, and most importantly, what they say.

Working Internally as an Actor and Writer

Many actors in America are trained in internal or psychological acting techniques. The Actors Studio, using the famous "method technique," bases a great deal of the work on the actor's personal life and his inner responses to the character on which he is working. Prior to having a character, writers can use some of these exercises to trigger their imagination to create one. This is, once again, like going to the other side of the mirror.

Writers can use some of the method techniques and exercises, and then combine what they discover with some improvisation work and imagination. By working sensorially, using their own memories, and then adding their imagination to the stew, writers can create all sorts of characters from a very personal place. Writers working this way aren't working from their head, but from their inner experiences and memories.

THE CHARACTER'S ACTIONS

Continuing to work internally like this, the writer can imagine how the character he's developed would respond in different situations. *The character's actions can be found by finding a single active present tense verb.* Writers must decide when creating (as do actors while rehearsing) what the character is doing (specific actions) at particular moments in the piece.

THE CHARACTER'S INTENTIONS

The character's intentions reveal what motivates the character, what he wants. Active verbs such as "I cherish" or "I regret" can reveal what the character wants at different times during the monologue or during the course of your monologue play. As you may recall from some of your acting classes, knowing the character's needs and knowing what motivates them is key to knowing how to play them. Knowing their needs is the first step to discovering what actions you must take to satisfy that need. This idea holds true for creating the characters on paper. Deciding what your character wants and what his goals are is the driving force in creating a fully realized character.

THE CHARACTER'S BIOGRAPHY

A character's biography tells you about your character's history. It can also reveal some of the motivating forces underlying your character's behavior. Actors/writers create in-depth biographies of the characters they're working on to give them deeper, more detailed information. The more you know about the character you're creating, the more you can reveal in the dialogue that you're writing. The way to find out biographical information on a character is by asking yourself as many questions as you can concerning the character. For instance:

- Where and when was I born?
- Did I have a happy childhood? What was it like?
- What were my parents like?
- What kind of house and neighborhood did we live in?
- How old was I, and what was it like the first time I fell in love?
- When was the first time I had sex? What was it like?
- What dreams do I remember from my childhood?

One key question that can conjure up all kinds of possibilities for your work is, "What if . . . ?" Perhaps you're familiar working with this question as an actor. The great acting teacher Konstantin Stanislavski used to require that his acting students answer a series of "What if . . ." questions while working on a character for a play. It was a way of allowing actors to imagine themselves in their character's shoes.

For instance, for work on *Romeo and Juliet*, the actor might ask himself "What if I was a prince who lived in Italy hundreds of years ago? And what if one day I fell in love with my father's worst enemy's daughter?" As you can see, these "What if . . ." questions are meant to fan the imagination. They allow you to wander away from your everyday world, into the imaginary world of the characters you're creating.

Asking yourself a series of "What if . . ." questions can help you develop themes for the monologue that you're working on. It can help you create deeper, more complex characters and give you ideas for situations that may be useful for your monologue. It's a form of theatrical role-playing that can get you into the situation that you're exploring. You'll find that you can jump-start a story, develop a character, or even create an entire monologue by using the "What if . . ." technique. Be adventurous and daring with your "What if . . ." questions. Don't censor or reject answers to your "What if . . ." questions because they momentarily might seem to have little value for the monologue you're working on. Let it take you as far as it can, and then, if necessary, later on, go back and rewrite.

Once your imagination has opened the door with "What if?" questions, continue your story by asking, "And then . . . ?" As with the "What if" technique, see where the "And then . . . " takes you. In the "What if?" phase, you set up an inquiry, an examination; you open up to an exploration. With "And then," you continue on your imaginary road, following your own lead, taking yourself wherever your imagination wants to go. These two phrases, when used together, can be very helpful tools in triggering the imagination.

STARTING TO WRITE

Inspiration

Webster defines inspiration as "To breathe in, to arouse. Communication of ideas from a supernatural source."

Two Scenarios

After you've done all the preparation, and are now ready to work, you may find yourself experiencing one of the two following scenarios.

SCENARIO 1: FREE FLOW, OUT IT COMES, I'M OFF, WHEEEE!!!

Some of you from the very get-go will find yourselves filling yellow pads or tapes with exciting material. You may be shocked at how much you have to say, how the material is just flowing out of you. You have suddenly discovered a floodgate opening, dialogue pouring out, characters emerging that you never even knew existed.

To some degree that was my experience when I first started writing character monologues about twelve years ago. Each morning when I sat down to write, I was amazed at how much came out. It was a nonstop roller coaster ride for many months. What amazed me at the time was that I was an actor; I thought of myself only as an actor. I'd never really written anything before, certainly not creatively. Where was all of this coming from? Who was this person sitting on my couch writing in such a frenzy? That writing spree went on day after day for nearly six months. During that time, I developed dozens of character monologues, which eventually led to the publication of my first book, *Street Talk: Character Monologues for Actors.*

If, when you first start out, that happens to you, my only advice is: Work every day for as long as you can. *Don't stop!* Keep going, every day! Also, don't throw anything away; file everything. If you're working on a computer, store everything. Congratulations, you've won the creative lottery. Enjoy it for as long as it lasts.

SCENARIO 2: HELP, I'M BLOCKED! THIS WRITING THING ISN'T WORKING!

Unfortunately, this second scenario also occurs to some just starting out (as well as experienced writers). Nothing seems to be happening. Nothing. Getting started feels futile. You're frustrated, bored, restless. You begin questioning your talent, your capability. You wonder why you're even bothering. You have all the symptoms of writer's block. It's a feeling that nothing is happening and probably never will. It can happen to anyone, at any time, but probably is most unsettling to those just starting out, who don't quite know the lay of the land yet. It's nothing to be alarmed about. Don't give up! It's not fatal, you won't die, don't panic. It's just a temporary condition. This too shall pass.

Understanding Writer's Block

Sometimes, to get to the really good creative stuff, or even get started, you have to clean out the exhaust pipe. Think of how in a car the exhaust pipe needs to be free to allow smoke and fumes out. It should never be blocked. Well sometimes our creativity feels like a blocked exhaust pipe. And the harder we try to force the smoke out, the worse it seems to get. We are plagued with doubts and negative thoughts such as: Who's going to care about this anyway? Am I really good enough? All artists deal with doubts like these all the time. I'm sure that you've dealt with them as an actor. Eventually you will learn to live with your doubts, and you will realize that self-censoring and insecurities are all part of the creative process.

One solution to the problem of writer's block is to realize that to get "there" (wherever it is you're hoping to go, creatively) you have to start with "here." And "here" is the room that you're in, with nothing on that paper, nothing on that tape, and no energy. You have to allow and accept the present moment. You have to live with the frustration that, indeed, nothing is happening. Just acknowledge it, try to live with it, and, when you're ready, move on.

An image that's been used to describe being creatively blocked is rocks in front of a cave. It may seem like there are some huge boulders blocking some magical creative cave. If only I could get behind those rocks, you think, I just know, *just know* there's some good creative stuff inside that cave. If only . . . if only . . . !

One of the great creative jokes is that sometimes the rocks that seem to be blocking the creative entranceway are, themselves, pure creative gold, the very stuff you've been looking for. But with all the effort to create, you didn't realize, couldn't see their value. They are the starting point! What I'm saying is that you have to start where you are. Start in the exact moment/place of your frustration or anger. What does that feeling do to you? What does it look like? How does it sound? Put it into words, write it down, put it into the character you're trying to create.

It all boils down to this: Don't work too hard, try to be easy on yourself, especially in the beginning. Once you get started, the momentum will pick up and soon you'll be on your way. Remember, whatever you go through, it's all part of the creative process, your creative process. When creating, trying to create, nothing's ever wasted.

Techniques for Dealing with Writer's Block

- Some writers say that, when experiencing writer's block, just writing anything, even copying a page out of a book, is one way that they get back into the groove of writing.
- Some monologists, when feeling blocked, will go see another monologist's or playwright's work. They say that just being in a theater and seeing good material can be quite inspiring.
- Keeping a pad around to jot down a thought or line of dialogue can also be a helpful aid during writer's block. One strong thought or image or some great line of dialogue can be just the trigger to get started.
- When working on a piece, some monologists purposely end each day's work in the middle of a sentence or thought. When they return the next day they can pick up the thread of where they left off and not have to look at an empty page.

Nothing, a Whole Lot of Nothing

And if all else fails and you find yourself sitting with writer's block, enjoy it. There's absolutely nothing wrong with just staring at the ceiling for a while. Yes, you read correctly. Stare at the ceiling or perhaps move those books around on the bookshelf (for the twelfth time), or give in to any slight diversion from doing your work. Meander, let your mind go, mentally wander. Yes, go ahead and avoid writing. Let yourself off the hook, obligation-wise. While sitting there, perhaps feeling frustrated, let your mind go wherever it wants. Give yourself permission to daydream, fantasize. This is one of the few times in life that it's not only okay, but perfectly appropriate. Remember back when you were in school and were bored? Back then you'd daydream all the time. What I'm talking about here is volitional daydreaming. Back in school no one ever had to give you permission to let your mind wander, right? It was an escape from the boredom. If you're feeling blocked, there's nothing wrong with some creative avoidance.

There's something very freeing about doing nothing, experiencing nothingness. Samuel Beckett wrote brilliant existential plays about nothingness. Larry David, the creator of *Seinfield*, the TV show, proved that something about nothing could become very popular (and lucrative). Perhaps, just perhaps, in the middle of your daydreaming, you may find a thought, a word, or a memory that stirs you to action, perhaps not. Let yourself off the hook, go fishing mentally.

Writing about Painful Events

One form of writer's block occurs when a writer tries to write about a painful event from his life that is still affecting him. You can't force yourself to write about something that is still too painful. Sometimes you have to wait until you have a manageable distance from the event to be able to exorcise it artistically. As with acting, writing should be organic. There must be a willingness and readiness to deal with the things that you want to express. Sometimes you just have to put those traumatic experiences on the back burner until you can find the right perspective.

Free-Writing: An Invaluable Exercise

Free-writing is probably the best way I know to start out on a new project. It can also be helpful in curing that writer's block. Free-writing is a method by which you put your pen to paper and write nonstop for at least ten minutes. It's a method for generating new ideas. With this method you allow ideas to lead you (rather than the other way around). When it's working well, one idea will ignite another. You'll be amazed at what and how much you have to say. This method is about quantity, not quality. This exercise is about first thoughts, impulses, anything that comes to mind. Quite often we squelch our impulses. This exercise helps you free yourself from that tendency. The only purpose of this exercise is to *keep writing nonstop for ten minutes!*

RULES TO FREE-WRITING

- Write as quickly as you can.
- Allow yourself to totally lose control while working.
- Don't stop to censor or revise anything.
- Don't stop to figure out what you've written; don't analyze it. Don't attempt to think or get logical about the words you've written.
- Pay no attention to spelling, grammar, or punctuation.
- Write all over the page, don't be concerned about margins or even the lines on the page.
- If you can't think of anything to write, then write about that.
- Don't cross out anything you've written.

- If something comes up that is embarrassing, painful, or frightening, quickly write it down.
- Take a sentence from what you've written, put it on the top of a page, then write for ten minutes about that sentence, using it as a topic sentence.

TAPE RECORDER USERS

Those of you working with tape recorders, adjust the exercise to nonstop talking (riffing). You can do this either standing or sitting, but most actors I know say they like to move around. The energy of working like this can take you all over the room, just go with any impulse that you have. You're not allowed to revise or censor anything.

BENEFITS OF FREE-WRITING

Free-writing instills discipline. It's a productive way to work through fears and anxieties about creating new material. Some writers use this method as a daily warm-up exercise before starting work on their piece. When you're working under pressure, it can jumpstart you into your day's work. Free-writing is also a useful tool that can give you ideas, help you learn to write effortlessly, more spontaneously. It can help to turn off that selfcensoring device that can be destructive, especially in the early stages of creating. By using free-writing you can train yourself to set deadlines and learn how to access that special energy that you need to meet them. It helps you learn to trust yourself as a creative artist and is a great way to view your stream of consciousness. The wonderful thing about this technique is that it not only helps with writer's block, but it also can reveal organized patterns of thought that are right below the surface.

AFTER A FREE-WRITING SESSION

Remember, this exercise is about process, not product. After you've done your freewriting session, look through the material to see if there is anything that you can use (a word, a phrase, some dialogue) for the project that you're presently working on. If there is, take it out. Then, immediately get rid of the rest of the free-writing work that you've done. The reason you do this is that sometimes there's a tendency to want to revise what you have on the page, using it as a first draft. As I've mentioned, that's not the idea of this exercise. It's not a first draft.

Here is a sample of one writer's free-writing work:

Here this is ridiculous. I can't . . . don't. What a waste. . . . I hope that I'm . . . Ridiculous. Crazy, I'm hoping, hopping, he held her at the dawn of light in the kitchen by the alcove under the kitchen sink with the plumber trying to fix the faucet. It wasn't broke, but it was her heart on her sleeve that really bothered the mailman on Monday after the cat came into the latrine. I'm not making any Look at them they know, they know what the story is really. Ridiculous is an absurd catch of the day by the fisherman on a Friday night because they're not allowed . . . Can't eat fish under the sink in retrospect my mother never made anything but pasta with sausage and lots of seasoning and my poodle named Sam would get up and eat it off the table and mama would cry at the sight of good food . . . is this ever going to end Probably on Tuesday in the mechanics shop, the car Anything. ANY-THING! Try to keep my mind I don't know. Keep it under your hat, loose lips sink cowboy hats under, a thunder at the door with a key in the open door-way . . . Tightly charged little men in the basement of the house without any warrant to arrest in the best behalf of some small characters in a novel by DeGaulle of the Parisian guard at the door to her hallway on a summer night where the breeze is nothing but a stye in the eye of anyone watching.

—by PATRICE JESTON

As you can see in this section of Patrice's free-writing sample, she let her sentences start and stop, didn't attempt to make sense of things, and let her thoughts unfold in any fashion. If you'll notice, she expresses her frustration about the exercise in some of the words she uses (and then moves on). As I've mentioned repeatedly, the main purpose of this exercise is to keep going no matter what. Later on, Patrice may discover a word or a line in her free-writing that evokes something that will give her an idea for a monologue. She may sift through the material and find something that conjures up a character that she may want to develop. I suggest that you try free-writing at least once a day as a warm-up before you start your day's writing work.

OPEN-IMPROVISING

Just to give some equal time to the improvisers, I'd like to mention the value of open-improvising (the improv version of free-writing) to warm up. Depending on how comfortable and adept you are at improvisation, it can be an extremely useful tool. You can work either with or without a tape recorder. Some actors find the tape recorder intimidating, saying it makes them feel like someone is watching them, judging them. Others say it frees them up to totally let go, knowing that they can play back the recording later to perhaps find tidbits that they can use in their work. Open-improvising is different than regular improvisation in that regular improv work is specifically focused on material, characters, or dialogue that you're working on. This is more free flowing, open ended.

Reread the above section on free-writing and wherever possible apply it to your open-improv riffing sessions. Don't forget to work for at least ten minutes. Let yourself go wherever you want in the room. Just start, say and do anything that comes to mind. Let your body become involved. Try not to become confined to any scenario or character. As one actor told me, "I just totally let myself lose my mind for a while. It's a great warm-up, really energizing and freeing."

Clustering (or Webbing): Finding the Initial Core of Your Work

Once you have prepared yourself, perhaps done the free-writing exercise, unless you're very clear about what you want to do and how you want to do it (and more specifically what you want to say), I suggest starting out with an excellent exercise called "clustering."

Clustering is a very popular writing method that was created by Gabrielle Lusser Rico and discussed in her book *Writing the Natural Way,* an excellent book for writers. Her technique helps you focus on what you're trying to say in your work. It utilizes the right side of the brain's ability to organize information. Sometimes when we start out on a new piece we may be overly enthusiastic, and we can't seem to find the root, the starting point, of where we want to go. And sometimes, even if we do know the starting point, it may be difficult to determine which areas of our work we need to focus on. Clustering helps you to find the through-line to your work. It helps you to zero in when too many thoughts and ideas seem to blur your creative landscape. Ironically, it's also useful when there's a lack of ideas.

Like free-writing, which it has similarities to, this technique helps you to bypass your conscious mind and get to your unconscious, perhaps the most creative part. The best way to describe clustering is "total free association" or "brainstorming."

How to Cluster

Start this exercise with a fresh sheet of paper. Write a word that is somehow connected to the monologue that you're about to start work on. Don't be concerned about which word you choose, whatever word comes to mind will do just fine. If you don't have a particular monologue in mind, or even have any ideas for one, just let any word that comes to mind be the one you choose.

Place the word in the middle of the page. Circle the word. Look at it for a moment. This core word or nucleus is the jumping-off point for the exercise.

Now as quickly as you can, allow yourself to free associate around your nucleus word, writing down as many words, images, short phrases, and bits of dialogue as you can. Each new word or phrase that you write down should radiate out from the nucleus word.

Draw circles around each new word or phrase. Link and connect similar ideas, phrases, bits of dialogue, etc. You can add arrows indicating direction if you wish.

If nothing spills out, doodle, putting arrows on your existing cluster. The doodling allows your hand to keep moving and may allow for possible associations to come to you.

Don't waste time trying to analyze anything, just go with your gut feelings. Don't stop until you have exhausted all possibilities. Keep going until you feel the need to write something. This shift will come in a thought like, "I've got it! I know what I want to write!"

Generally most writers work with clusters for up to a few minutes. When you feel compelled to write, start immediately! Don't give yourself time to get back in your head. Start writing as fast as you can.

If nothing particular inspires you to write, then look at the words or phrases in the cluster and select any one of them. Start writing about that word or phrase. As you start writing, you'll probably notice a connection of ideas stemming from the word. Keep writing for at least ten minutes if you can. You can refer back to the cluster if you wish.

Remember, there is no right or wrong here. This should just be thought of as an exercise. Between five and ten minutes into this speed writing there should be some effort to reach closure. Don't force it.

Here is an example of a cluster group exercise I did that eventually lead to the creating of a monologue.

I began with the core word: "Mars." I circled the word and let my mind free-associate. I kept going for almost three minutes. Here is just a sampling of some of the many words that I came up with. I circled, linked, and connected them.

> *yellow, tea, coffee! Help . . . fight . . . ugly . . . creepy! America . . . wired . . . scared . . . kill . . . run . . . fight, flag, kill, God . . . man . . . day . . . go . . . beat . . . proud . . . See . . . Everyone . . . Told ya. Out . . . get out!! . . . Zoom! . . . Smile . . . . Yes . . . Yes!!*

After looking at the group of circled and linked words for just a moment, I began what turned out to be the first draft of a monologue, which eventually became the following piece.

Sal from *Street Talk: Character Monologues for Actors* by Glenn Alterman

He wanted home-fried potatoes, that's all. I don't know, I remember, he came in here lookin' like anybody else. Short guy, sat at the counter. Right over there. I asked him, "Yeah, what'll it be?" And he said, "Home-fried potatoes." Nothing unusual, no big deal. So I ordered up with Sam, my short order cook. And I turn around and this guy's like smiling. Not unusual. But . . . there's like this green glow comin' offa him. Yeah. That's the best way I can put it. Right then and there I knew somethin' strange was happenin'. Now listen, we get all kinds comin' in here. Two, three in the morning, we get truckers, drag queens, hookers, but none of 'em, none of 'em ever glows with green rays comin' out of 'em.

So, I kept it together, said, "Excuse me . . . um, is there somethin' else I can get'cha . . . besides the potatoes?" And he stopped smilin'. He was like starin'. Intense. Like he was studying me or something. He looked at me like

... like I was some kina insect. Creepy. Very creepy! If I wasn't the only one behind the counter, shit I woulda jumped and ran. But the boss woulda killed me for leavin' the register.

Now there were a couple of regulars at the counter, drinkin' their coffee, oblivious to the whole thing. Whereas I was freaked! I never seen anybody glow. Ever! And it kept gettin' brighter and brighter. I was trying to keep my composure, but I was fallin' apart.

Then, we get like into this starin' match. Him and me. And even though he's not sayin' anything I can hear his thoughts. Yeah. An' he was sayin' some weird shit. Stuff like a computer. Yeah. Like "the population of New York is . . . The size of the city . . . Elected officials are . . . " All this data shit.

And I'm gettin' so scared I think I'm gonna shit in my pants. I don't know what to do. Should I call 911? My wife? My mother? The army? An' this guy's glow is gettin' brighter and brighter. Takin' over the whole diner! This green shit's coverin' everything!

Finally I say, "Hey mister, your fries should be ready in a minute. You want something to drink, like coffee or somethin'?"

Then he screams in this high pitched tone, "Coffee?! Cof-feee?! You mean caffeine? Caf-feeine?!"

I said, "Uh, . . . uh we got decaffeinated if you like, or tea . . . or somethin'. I don't know."

Then his green shit gets brighter, and floods the place! Guys at the counter they fell over backwards. I figured they was dead.

I lost it, screamed, "Mama-mia, what are you doin' mister?! Ya food'll be ready in a minute. Please stop, please!"

Then the whole diner starts to shake. Yeah. Like it was an earthquake. Dishes flyin' all over the fuckin' place. Sam comes runnin' out of the kitchen, screamin', "What the hell . . . !" but when he sees this guy, he turns and runs back in, leavin' me alone, face to face with it! Whatever it was.

And then, then his face starts contorting in these weird ways, like it's made of rubber. It's mouth opens wide, and out comes this long, pointy yellow tongue. And this tongue starts comin' at me. Long and pointy and sharp. And the place is shakin' like crazy. . . .

Finally, I totally freaked! I said, "Enough! Enough! Get that fuckin' tongue back in your mouth and get the hell out of here! Now! Who the hell you think you are?!" I felt so strong. Like I wanted to wave a flag or somethin'. At first, nothin' happened. But then the place stopped shakin' and calmed down. My heart was racin' like crazy, but I stood there locked, with my fists like clenched. Then I pointed to the door and said, very softly, "Get out."

And the green rays zapped back into his body. An' he pulled that tongue of his back in. His face stopped contortin', and he looked like anybody else.

But then he kina slumped over in his seat, looked dejected or somethin'.

He put a buck on the counter for the home fries, which he never got, an' said, almost in a whisper, "Thank you. Thank you very much sir." And he started to leave.

I stood there, still shakin', an' said, "Sure. You're welcome. You're welcome." An then . . . he left.

BEGINNING YOUR MONOLOGUE: STRUCTURE AND PROCESS

Before actually starting work on your monologue, I suggest that you create an outline, perhaps based on some information learned during the free-writing or clustering sessions. This outline should be much more detailed than the preliminary one that you did earlier. The purpose of this outline is to serve as a road map for your work.

Write out, in as much detail as possible, the story that you plan on telling. If it's a short character monologue, describe the character physically, listing personality traits, desires, quirks, etc. If it's a character that's speaking conversationally either to someone else or to the audience directly, you might want to write out the story of the piece in narrative form first.

If it's an autobiographical monologue, pinpoint important moments, dates, details, and a rough outline of the story line. You should begin with a general sense of how you want the piece to go, that is, where it'll start and where it will end. It's better at this point to have an abundance of information, much of which you may not use.

If it's a reality-based monologue, line up your facts, dates, and characters. Since this material is factual in nature, accuracy and specifics are very important. You may need to arrange tape-recorded interviews. You should start thinking about the tone and form that you want the piece to take. Anna Deavere Smith's *Fires in the Mirror* has a documentary style feel to it. She recreated the people that she interviewed, using their exact words to tell her story.

If it's a performance art piece, list some of the ideas that you have in mind for the presentation. What form do you see it having? What audiovisual material will you need? Will you be using dance, songs? Will you need to secure the rights for any materials? Describe the piece as you see it in your mind. What is it that you're hoping your piece will say to an audience? You don't need to intellectually explain it, just tell why you are writing it; what's your point?

Write down any ideas or suggestions that you feel eventually may be helpful in creating your monologue. List all the potential characters that might be a part of your story. Give some thought to how you would like to develop them. List any scenes or locations that you might include.

Outline the journey (where you want to take your audience) of your piece as you now see it. Write the story out in a narrative form.

Remember, this is still just a preliminary overview; things will probably change (maybe even substantially) as you go along. You're not married to any of the ideas, images, or characters.

How We'll Be Working from Now On

Because we are dealing with so many different types of monologues, I'll mainly be discussing the work in process terms. I'm sure that you'll be able to see where your particular piece fits in as we go along. Since each solo artist progresses at a different pace, I'll discuss the work in small increments.

Now that you've done all the preliminary "head" work, thinking, structuring, perking, and planning, the only thing that remains is the actual doing, the writing, the creating of your monologue.

Comparing the Actor's And Writer's Processes of Starting Out

During that first read of a new play, you, the actor, (hopefully) have no preconceived ideas of what your character will be about or how you will go about creating him. It's a very vulnerable, open time in an actor's creative process. It's a time of taking in, reading the script, digesting the information, and then preparing to respond creatively to what you've read.

After that initial reading of the play, you have feelings and ideas about the character you are about to create. Creative juices are flowing, the imagination is at work. Starting with some initial impulses, you begin thinking of ways you will go about creating your new character.

At the beginning of a new monologue or monologue play, you, the writer, are opening a door for yourself. From the very first lines you write, you are taking yourself somewhere, although you may not be quite sure where yet. The more spontaneous you can allow yourself to be, the more personal and original your work will be.

The outline that you've created can serve as a sort of skeletal script, giving you a sense of direction of where you might want to go on this journey. The more you can *surprise yourself,* especially here at the beginning, the more exciting the ride will be both for you and the audience.

Both actors and writers begin at a similar point, a place of vulnerability, openness, potential. Anything can happen; the sky's the limit!

The Importance of the Narrator

In many monologues, there is a narrator who takes us through the journey of the piece. In autobiographical material, it can be the character representing the author; in an evening of character monologues, it may be the person who ties all the characters and/or the story (or stories) together.

In performance art pieces, it can be the performance artist himself, telling the story as he wants to tell it. We (the audience) should like or identify with the narrator in some way. At the very least, we should be interested in listening to what he has to say.

If the narrator is written as an unlikable character, a villain (like Salieri in *Amadeus* or the M.C. in *Cabaret*), the audience must find something that is intriguing or fascinating about him. It's helpful if you can find some captivating detail of his personality that allows us to see the world through his (perhaps) distorted point of view. We have to trust or be intrigued by the narrator, or at the very least believe that what he is telling us is true (at least true to him). If we don't believe him, or can't follow his thinking, we'll lose interest early on in the monologue.

THE ROLE OF THE NARRATOR IN MONOLOGUES

As I've mentioned, generally the narrator is at the core of certain monologues or monologue plays. It's important to decide, early on, what role you want the narrator to have in your piece. Here are just a few suggestions.

- Does he represent the neutral, calm voice of reason?
- Is he the protagonist?
- Is he that cynical voice that we all have at one time or another?
- Is he the patient teacher, educating the audience?
- Is he the injured party, the victim?
- Is he an everyman that most people will relate to?

Your Opening Section: The First Paragraphs

The opening section of your monologue is quite important. It's your diving-off point. It's your welcome mat to your audience. It's the "once upon a time" element that invites your audience to sit down with you for a while and listen to what you have to say. Your monologue should begin where it needs to begin—for you. It should start where your story has to start—for you. The beginning of your monologue is your foundation, the base where the rest of the piece will stem from. It should hint at, if not actually state, where you're going with the rest of the piece.

It's especially important, while working on the beginning, not to censor or stifle any images or ideas. Your monologue starts from anywhere it needs to start. Don't become too preoccupied with how effective your opening is.

You'll find that openings and closings of monologues are the parts that generally receive the most rewrites. Once you've completed the entire monologue and know what it's about, then you can go back and see if the beginning and ending need further rewrites.

GIMMICKY OPENINGS

Try not to manipulate the opening section of your monologue "for effect," to get a rise from your audience. Gimmicky beginnings, unless honestly organic to the story, usually come off as desperate ploys by insecure writers to get an audience's attention. If your opening needs to start out with something shocking, something that's germane to your story, then by all means do so. But that's very different than just arbitrarily opening your piece with some obvious attention getting device like loud noises or flashing lights, just for effect.

Here are some examples of opening sections of monologues.

From *Charlotte* by Penny Arcade (from *True Stories*, Performance Space 122, 1989)

I'm wearing a wig! I have to. I had a face-lift. Well, I had to. Well, I had to work. See I figured I could work four or five years if I got my face done. You know my friend Sandra, the big blonde? Well she had her eyes done up here in New York, and that costs her twenty-five hundred dollars. Well, I did not have that kind of money. But I know this gal, she used to be a madam up here in New York, but she retired to Caracas. She's real well connected down there, you know diplomats and all. Now she told me I could go down there, stay at her house, and use her doctor. She has a beautiful home there. They call that a villa. Now the only thing that she did not tell me was that her doctor worked at a teaching hospital. They gave me the face-lift of an 80-year-old woman!

From the opening lines, we get a sense of who this character is (or may be). By the author's use of an exclamation point at the end of the first sentence, we can feel an energy, an immediacy to Charlotte's character. What she has to say seems very important to her and therefore engages us.

As she continues to speak, we learn of her situation, a bit of where she's at in her life, her style of speaking, even what's important to her at this time, and why. That's a lot of information in under twenty lines. Ms. Arcade chose a conversational style for her character's dialogue. You feel like the character is talking directly to you. Using this conversational form in monologue writing is one way to engage an audience.

From *Michael* by Glenn Alterman (from *Uptown*)

I kept, hopin', y'know? Kept . . . For months. But I knew. I just . . . Losing weight, tired all the time. Mom kept sayin', "Mickey, you're getting' so thin. What's wrong, tell me." Told her, "s'nothin' ma, just stress, don't worry about it." Telling myself, it's this or that. Any excuse, one after another. But then I ran out of things, y'know? No reasons left. So finally I went to the doctor—took the test.

From the very opening lines, we get a sense of Michael's anxiety, his concern about some possible health dilemma. He mentions that his mother has been worrying about him, that he too is concerned. The suspense of what's wrong with him is the device that brings us into his situation. We become involved in his story, want to know how it'll be resolved. That's the setup for this monologue.

Who the actor is speaking to is something that must be addressed. In this case, the phrase "Mom kept sayin'" makes us assume that Michael is speaking to a relative, probably a sibling. If, based on specific clues in the dialogue, the actor decides that he's speaking to a friend, the action and tone will be very different than if he's speaking to a group of other patients in a hospital. The writer should indicate somewhere in the text who the listener is.

Starting a monologue with a question (to a still unidentified listener) is one way of drawing us into the character's world, his situation. The style that I used for this monologue is conversational. We are immediately brought into the character's reality. We feel that we're a part of the drama.

From *Swimming to Cambodia* by Spalding Gray

It was the first day off in a long time, and all of us were trying to get a little rest and relaxation out by the pool at this big, modern hotel that looked something like a prison. If I had to call it anything I would call it a "pleasure prison." It was the kind of place you might come to on a package tour out of Bangkok. You'd come down on a chartered bus—and you'd probably not wander off the grounds because of the high barbed-wire fence they have to keep you in and the bandits out. And every so often you would hear shotguns going off as the hotel guards fired at rabid dogs down along the beach on the Gulf of Siam.

Gray opens his autobiographical monologue with a description of the hotel in Cambodia that he stayed at during the shooting of the film, *The Killing Fields.* He is setting the scene, recalling his impressions of the place. He uses the narrative form. We learn quite a bit about Gray from the descriptive words he uses, his feelings about where he was. Calling his hotel a "prison" and then a "pleasure prison" gives you an insight as to how he viewed his surroundings. By mentioning "barbed wire fences" and "guns going off in the distance," Gray chooses images that begin to take us into the world in which he was living.

From *Pretty Fire* by Charlayne Woodard

One day, when Allie and I were watching old black and white movies, Mommy walked into the living room and turned off the TV. She said, "Ladies, tell me what would you like to be when you grow up?"

(Raising her hand) "Me first, Mommy, me first! (Standing) I want to be ... Lassie. Yes, Mommy, I want to run through the field and jump over the fence, and see ... the little girl ... trapped in the mine ... and I will call for help!" (Barking) Arf, arf, arf, arf, arf arf! And evening will come and they will save that little girl trapped in the mine. Then they'll say, 'Good girl, Lassie. (Reacting to her neck being petted as if she's a dog) Good girl, Lassie ...' And Mommy, they will love me!"

The opening words, "One day, when Allie and I were watching old ... ," is similar in effect to the "Once upon a time" style opener for many stories we've all heard growing up. Its friendliness and informality immediately invite you to come inside and enjoy listening to the story. Ms. Woodard's autobiographical character monologue begins with a reminiscence about an event in her childhood. There is a friendly, warm tone to the piece. Notice that she doesn't say, "my mother," but rather uses the word, "Mommy." See how that affects the tone of her storytelling.

By "present tensing" the dialogue in her story, the event takes on an immediacy. We get a sense that the past is momentarily occurring in the present. Present tensing can be very effective when you're repeating dialogue from the past.

Ms. Woodard's monologues are written in well-drawn vignettes. She brings to life not only assorted incarnations of herself, but also other family members and people from the neighborhood. Her stories are funny, poignant, and tragic. She has the ability to crawl into the skin of her many characters without letting us see her tracks.

Blanka from *Some People* by Danny Hoch

(Blanka, a young twenty-ish office worker stops by her friend's house to borrow shoes.)

Listen Linette, lemme borrow your shoes? The short black ones. No because Manny gets off Footlocker in twenty minutes and I have to take the bus. But I can't be looking ugly in the bus. So find them! Don't stress me more alright? My life is already stressed enough, can I tell you? The other day right? I was at Manny's house, and we was fooling around, and like you know how guys be getting all shy like when they wanna say something really important but they don't say it? Or like they say it, but like their voices be getting all low so you can't hear what they saying? So he was doing that right, and I don't like playing that. I was like, hello-excuse-me-I-can't-hear-you-what-you-saying-right?

Danny Hoch writes mainly urban, character monologues. The form of writing Hoch uses is conversational dialogue. He opens this particular monologue with the character Blanka engaged in a conversation with her friend, Linette. We become eavesdroppers listening to Blanka speaking. We quickly learn personal information about Blanka by her choice of words and her unique manner of speaking. We learn about her sense of herself and how she feels about Manny, her boyfriend.

DEVELOPING
YOUR MONOLOGUE

L et's assume at this point that you're satisfied with the opening section of your monologue. Allow yourself to move on, using the outline and opening section as a diving board for new ideas, images, and dialogue. Once again, it's not necessary to always know exactly where you're going with the monologue. Now it's really just a matter of trusting your instincts and impulses and allowing them to propel you forward, letting your imagination guide you. At this point, the most important thing is to just keep going.

Developing Your Role (as an Actor)

This early stage of developing your monologue can be compared to a similar stage in an actor's process. In rehearsal you start saying the lines in the script to the other actors. One line of dialogue leads to the next, you go from action to action. The other actor responds to you, and you respond to him, and so it goes. You know where the play ends, but now you have to explore, to see where your character fits into each scene. At this point in the actor's process, you're not (or shouldn't be) limiting yourself in any way. It's a time to *fly and try*.

Developing Your Monologue (as a Writer)

Similarly, as a writer, this also is a time when you should allow impulses and ideas to lead you. Let yourself be both the leader and the follower. If what you're writing makes you smile or laugh, assume that it's funny, and that an audience will also laugh. If it makes you cry, trust that it will have the same effect on an audience.

Don't try to second-guess or manipulate anything. This is also not the time to over-analyze or revise anything you've written so far. It's a time of moving forward at your own pace, letting each section unfold into the next section, each creative segment melt into the next one. Remember, any rewrites can always be done later on.

The Ongoing Day-to-Day Work

Your work continues until you've completely told the story that you wanted to tell. You shouldn't be too concerned at this time about particular sections along the way that may not quite be there yet. At this point it's really more important to get the story down. That doesn't mean that you should be rushing to get to the end of a first draft; take your time; enjoy yourself.

If you feel an impulse to travel off course, away from the outline you created, go there, try it, see where it takes you. You can always backtrack later and return to your original ideas. Sometimes those great surprises that you come up with while traveling off course become the unusual twists and turns that make a monologue most memorable. This should be a time of experimenting, writing impulsively, wandering wherever you want to go.

It's important to try to work every day, even if it's just for a half hour. When you're not working on your piece, it's usually a good idea to have a pad and pen around to jot down ideas or dialogue that may suddenly come to you during the day. One thing you'll start to realize is that your subconscious mind is always working on your monologue, even when you're not consciously thinking about it. Some of the most inspired moments and best lines of dialogue occur when you're sitting on a bus going uptown, or watching TV. If an idea comes to you, simply take out your pad and pen and write it down. I'm sure that as an actor, while working on a role, these inspired insights also occurred when you weren't actually rehearsing.

While working on short character monologues, audition pieces, etc., don't be concerned about how long the piece is running. Even if it's running pages longer than you originally intended, keep going. Later on, in rewrites, you can always trim the piece down.

With larger pieces such as monologue plays, performance art pieces, etc., some writers prefer working in chunks or sections of the play, dividing it into acts. When they feel they have a substantial amount of material, they'll revise what they have, then go on to the next chunk of material, etc.

Other writers (most that I spoke to) prefer to go the whole route, continuing until they finish a complete first draft of the entire play. Then they'll backtrack, doing rewrites on various sections as needed. Once again, whatever works best for you is the best way.

When working on an evening of character monologues, each monologue can be thought of as a separate block and should be worked individually. Naturally you need to keep in mind the thread that ties all the pieces together. This may be a group of neighbors, a common theme, a story line, etc. But don't let that device restrict you in any way; you don't want an evening of individual character monologues where all the characters are too similar.

Working on Performance Art Pieces

Performance art pieces, as I've mentioned previously, don't follow many of the same rules as other monologues. They allow for a freer creative style. Certain things, however, that you should keep in mind when working on performance art monologues are:

- How do you plan on telling your story? What form do you think it will take? Do you plan on using dance? Visuals? Music? Lighting? Poetry?
- What ideas are you trying to express? What are you trying to say?
- Describe, in as much detail as you can, the theatrical journey on which you hope to take your audience.

Some performance artists that I spoke with prefer not to use an outline of any kind. They feel that they are too constricting. When they begin work on a new piece, they may have just an idea or image in mind. They develop the piece in sections, working moment to moment, allowing their ideas or images to lead them into the form that the piece eventually takes.

A Word about Songs, Music, and Dance in Monologue Plays

Some monologists like to incorporate songs and music and dance into their monologue plays. This is especially true in performance art pieces. If used well, music and dance can certainly enhance written material and showcase an actor's musical ability. I suggest though that you only use them if you feel they will add something not already said in your text. They should be thought of as a sort of seasoning, and shouldn't overpower the text (unless that's your specific intention).

Another matter to take into consideration is their legality. If you write your own songs or music, obviously there's no problem. If, however, you want to use someone else's copyrighted material, you'll need to get their permission first (and perhaps pay royalties). The same is true of using text from other sources. For example, Mary Louise Wilson had to get the rights to the book *D.V.* before she could begin work on her play *Full Gallop.*

Mixed Media

To visually enhance their performances, many monologists use slide projections, art-work, and so on, as an aid in expressing what they're trying to say. If using visuals is something that you wish to explore in your work, fine. Just one word of caution: Be care-ful; don't overdue. Always keep in mind that you're just one person alone on a stage per-forming. The more visuals you use, the more the audience's focus will be divided. If that's your intention, then go ahead. But in general, in monologue plays, less is more. Sometimes, out of insecurity, the monologist (or his director) overdoes the visuals, lessening the effect of the monologue itself.

That Old Devil, the Self-Censor

One interfering monster that you may come up against is the self-censor. The self-censor is that judging, criticizing spoiler inside our heads that stops the rhythm of what we're doing by making negative comments. It happens at different times to all artists. There is no way to avoid it; it comes with the territory. Some writers have the ability to ignore it; others are temporarily stymied by it. How you learn to deal with your own self-judging, self-criticizing, is a valuable part of your creative process. I'm sure that as an actor, from time to time, that same judging voice interfered with your work on developing or performing a role. The only thing that you can do is acknowledge what it is and keep working, trying not to let it interfere or overwhelm you. The more confident you become as a writer the less it will affect you.

Taking Mini-Breaks, Breathers

Keep writing or improvising nonstop for as long as your energy and stamina hold up. Some monologists can only work for about twenty or thirty minutes before they feel they need a break. Others can work for many hours nonstop. You'll know instinctively when it's time for you to break.

While working on material, occasionally you go through dry patches, or what seems like a temporary stop in the creative flow. It feels like you've run out of ideas. This is generally one of those times to take a breather. Relax, stop what you're doing, and temporarily do something else.

During a break, I'll get up, leave the work area, perhaps go into another room. I try to get my mind momentarily off what I'm doing. Sometimes you just need a good stretch, perhaps a brief walk outside in the fresh air. I'll listen to music for a few min-utes or maybe make myself a light snack (preferably a healthy one) or a cup of coffee. Any short distraction will work, as long as you keep your mind off the monologue.

You may find that while you're recouping, fresh ideas related to the material start coming to you. If that occurs, fine, simply jot down whatever insight or dialogue came to you, and continue on with what you're doing. Don't give these new ideas too much thought at this point. When you feel refreshed, go back to the work area and pick up where you left off. Hopefully you'll feel recharged, ready to continue work.

Looking Over What You've Written So Far

After the break, I usually browse over what I've written so far. My main purpose in reviewing material is to get me back into the groove of where I was before the break. It's important not to judge or censor what you've written so far. If you can, resist revising anything. Revising puts your mind into an analytical mode, something that we're not up to yet. The idea at this point is to continue onward, not to backtrack or clean up roads you've already passed through.

After the Break: Two Scenarios

And so you continue working in the same way that you were prior to your break. You may notice that you suddenly have fresh ideas, have a new outlook, are able to look at the material from a new point of view. If that's the case, the break was successful.

If, however, you're still creatively dry, you have two options. You can either take another break, or more advisable, work through the dry patch. Periods of mental lethargy can be frustrating, I know. But many times it comes out of a psychological avoidance of something within the material. If you can, push through, try to find out what's on the other side of the resistance. Once you get there, things will flow a lot smoother.

Working 'til the End of the First Draft

Continue working on your monologue until there is nothing more to say, until you feel you've completely told your story. In the case of character monologues, you should feel that each of the monologues has a workable beginning, middle, and end. You should have a feeling of completion, accomplishment. That's not to say that there won't be sections, lines of dialogue, and even characters that you know still need further work. But that should not short-change your feeling of accomplishment after completing the first draft of your monologue. Enjoy the moment, and then give yourself a well-deserved break.

DEVELOPING YOUR MONOLOGUE II (THE ONGOING WORK)

At this point, we're about to begin the craft part of the work. You're about to shift from the creative mode of inspiration and creation to the more analytical one. To begin this process, you have to reread the entire first draft with a different mind-set than when you were creating it.

The "Who Wrote This Monologue, and What's It About?" Exercise

One way to approach the first read through of your material is an exercise called "Who Wrote This and What's It About?" It's a way of separating yourself from your work and reading the manuscript with a fresh perspective. Rather than just picking up the script and reading it straight out, try playing this little game with yourself. When you sit down to look at the manuscript, pretend that you didn't write it. Pretend that you're seeing those words on the pages for the very first time. If you're listening to a tape-recorded first draft, pretend that you've never heard those words before. Pretend that you don't know anything about the author of the piece. As you're reading, jot down *anything* that seems unclear to you. If you have any questions about any specific section, character, or idea, just jot them down as you go along. The idea is to pretend that you're a member of the audience, a critic, a person with a very discerning, critical mind.

I know that at first it may feel a little strange trying to pretend you've never seen this script that you've been working on for however long. But this exercise can be very helpful. The more objective you can be during the first read through, the more efficient the rewrite process may be later on. You'll also find this to be an interesting (if not unusual) acting task.

Questions to Ask Yourself while Reading through Your Script

Whether or not you decide to use the "Who Wrote This . . . ?" exercise, here are some important questions you should try to keep in mind while reading through your monologue (play). You should refer to these questions periodically, also using them as guidelines during subsequent read throughs.

- Does the script engage you? The moment you feel disengaged, just mark the passages, then continue reading. Don't analyze or try to fix anything at this point.
- Do you find the story interesting, easy to follow? If not, where does it go off? Mark those sections. Again, don't try to fix anything.
- Wherever you feel the story of the monologue loses you (becomes too convoluted, confusing), mark the section.
- About the characters: Do you believe them? Do all the characters seem fully realized? If not, at which point do you feel they lose you? Be as specific as you can, underline the line or moment.
- Does the way each character speaks sound authentic? Mark the words or passages that sound false.
- If there are multiple characters in the piece, do any of them seem too similar to other characters?
- Do you care about these characters? Do they offend you, annoy you, seem too abrasive, seem too sentimental?
- If this is a multiple character piece, do you feel that all the characters are interesting? Necessary? Can any of the characters be combined?
- Do you feel at any point that there's too much narrative or exposition? Always keep in mind that this monologue will be performed, not read.
- Do you notice any repetition in the dialogue, the same words or phrases being overused? Keep in mind that in everyday use, there are certain colloquial expressions that people do use repeatedly. Does the repetition make your dialogue sound authentic and specific, or does it just sound like sloppy writing?
- Do you feel that there is a repetition in the ideas being expressed? Are some characters expressing the same ideas repeatedly?
- Is it clear what the writer is trying to say in this piece?

- How do you feel after finishing the piece? Did you find it satisfying? Do you wish there was more? Do you feel that there was too much of any one element, character, scene, and so on?

At What Point Should You Have Someone Else Read What You've Written?

This is a very tricky question. Many writers want to get feedback on their monologue as soon as they've finished working on the first draft. Getting it to someone for a response at the right time can be very helpful. But getting it to a reader prematurely can be damaging to your process, your future work on the piece. Once you let others into the stew, so to speak, they become a part of your relationship with your own material. Their input, comments, and suggestions will have an impact on your future rewrites. You may want to wait until the second or third draft before handing it over to someone else for input. There is no rule on this; only you will know when the time is right. The best rule of thumb here is to give it to someone else to look at when you honestly feel that you've done as much work on it as you possibly can for the time being.

Selecting the Right Person to Read Your Monologue

Whom you ask to read your manuscript is very important. You should trust and respect the opinion of the person that you're asking to read your material. You should feel that he can intelligently articulate any problems that he sees in your text. It's a very vulnerable time for you as the writer of the script. You need to make sure that the person you've asked to criticize your piece is someone who will be honest with you, but also supportive. And always remember, no matter who you choose, he is just one person, with his own subjective point of view; he's not God. At the end of the day, it's always your opinion that carries the most weight.

I personally feel that writers should hold off as long as they can before handing their work over to someone else for criticism. Try to give yourself as much time as you need, live with your script for as long as you can. Only give it to someone else when you honestly feel that you can no longer be objective about it or feel that there are large problems that you just can't get a handle on. Do not expect or ever allow the reader that you've selected to give you solutions to problems that he sees or suggestions as to how you should rewrite your monologue. The best readers are the ones that can pose the right questions to you, not give you answers.

Performing the First Draft for a Director

As to whether you should perform the first draft of your monologue for a director for feedback, again, that's your call. If it's the director whom you've selected to direct your play, it can certainly be helpful to have him included early on in the process. (See "Selecting a Director" in chapter 14.) As I have previously mentioned, quite often, one of the functions of directors of solo shows is that of dramaturge. It's also an opportunity for you both to see how comfortable you feel working with each other. If you have a particular director that you're thinking of developing the piece with, discuss with him which way he feels would work best for the two of you.

Performing the First Draft as a "Work in Progress" for an Audience

Some monologists prefer to develop material in front of an audience early on. After the first draft or two, they begin performing it for small groups as a work in progress, making their revisions based on the audiences' nightly responses to their work. The audience may be a few friends in a living room or a paying audience in a small club or theater. Letting the audience know in advance that this is still a work in progress lowers the audience's level of expectation. Some audiences enjoy seeing works in progress because they feel that they're contributing to the monologist's process. After each performance there's a question and answer session where the audience can make comments about the work they've seen. Their comments can be very helpful to the monologist and the director of the piece.

Making Repairs: Rewriting

Successful monologue writing (actually all writing) relies heavily on rewriting. That first inspired batch of material may feel complete, but always be ready and willing, at any time, to revise, rewrite, perfect. That's not to say that sometimes you can't get it right that first time out. That does happen, but generally most writers, playwrights, and performance artists that I've spoken to think of their early work, that first draft, as "fodder, raw material." You should look forward to chiseling away at your work until it expresses exactly what you're trying to say at every given moment. Never settle, never rush, never compromise.

Revising and Reshaping

One of the most important aspects of the rewriting process is revising and reshaping your text. The more you understand what you've written, more specifically, what you're trying to say (at any given moment), the more you'll know precisely what needs editing or further developing. The first stage of revising is similar to cleaning out your closet. As you look through it, you realize that some things are unnecessary and can be thrown out. Eventually new clothes will be bought and added to your wardrobe, filling up your closet again. Only you can decide what remains and what goes. And only you can decide what new clothes you want to buy.

The Three Golden Rules of Revising

1. Eliminate any *words* that don't relate to the *main idea* of the sentence
2. Eliminate those *sentences* that don't relate to the *main idea* of the paragraph
3. Eliminate the *paragraphs* that don't relate to the *main idea* of your monologue

What follows is a question and answer section pertaining to techniques for revising and reshaping monologues.

Are there sections that seem extraneous to the story?

Part of the job in writing monologues is learning how to best tell your story. Unfortunately, sometimes monologue writers fall in love with their own dialogue or refuse to cut a beautiful phrase or a colorful word because they like the sound of it or the image it evokes. To make your story clear, you sometimes have to sacrifice. Monologues are meant to be performed. Extraneous dialogue can weigh your story down and bore your audience. Be succinct in your storytelling. Get to the point and then move on.

Are there any sections that need to be opened up, further developed?

On the other end of the storytelling spectrum is not giving your audience enough information. This usually happens when there is more going on in the writer's head than he has put down on the page. The writer's thoughts are not yet being fully expressed; the story is not being completely told. The bottom line on this is: If it's not on the page, it's not on the stage. It's always easier to write the material and cut back if it turns out that you are over-explaining.

When you become aware (either by your own reading or through feedback from other readers) that a particular section needs further development, try to trace your steps back to where the confusion began. At that juncture, pick up where you left off, working to reveal, to open up, what's missing in that moment (through the use of dialogue or narrative). Continue working that way until you've opened it up as much as you can. Then, later on, perhaps during subsequent read throughs, return to the section and see if it needs to be pared down, if perhaps you've overwritten it.

It's the constant back-and-forth revisions to the section that will reveal the clearest truth of what you're trying to say. The rule of thumb here is: Only say what must be said, nothing more and nothing less.

Here are some questions that you can ask yourself to find out if a particular section of your monologue needs further development:

- Have I referred to places, people, or events in my monologue that the audience may not be aware of?
- In general, does my audience have enough background information on the story that I'm trying to tell them? Could I give them some more exposition?

- Have I made a strong enough case for the idea that I'm trying to get across to the audience?
- Have I taken into account possible arguments or problems that members of the audience may have with my ideas? If so, what is the best way for me to answer their objections in advance?

Are there too many characters in the monologue?

Always keep in mind that your monologue will only be performed by one actor, you. Having unnecessary characters in your piece will only add to your creative burden as an actor and, ultimately, to the audience's confusion. Certain characters may be too similar; combining them will make your story sharper, clearer. Also, multiple characters revealing the same information tend to "bloat" the monologue. Try combining them into a single character who can more effectively be the messenger of the story you're trying to tell.

Are there too many stories in my monologue (monologue play)?

Any of the longer monologue plays (autobiographical, narrative, etc.) can handle several intermeshing subsidiary stories. But try to avoid having too many complex stories with unnecessary characters. If you do so, your audience will lose the impact of the main story and/or the ideas that you're trying to express. If possible, try to somehow connect or funnel the subsidiary stories, having them relate to or resonate from your main story or idea(s).

As for an evening of character monologues, try not to hamper the individual monologues with too many stories or overfill them with too many characters. That's not saying that the monologues taken together can't spin a complex and layered yarn, just try to tell each part of the story with clarity and simplicity.

Does my monologue go off on tangents? Does my story meander? Am I repeating myself?

As I have mentioned earlier, keeping your story focused and succinct are two of the most important aspects of successful monologue writing. Long-winded and unyielding stretches of dialogue or narrative don't play well in performance. A character or narrator who talks endlessly on the same subject quickly wears out his welcome. As you read through your monologue, look to see if you're repeating yourself too often. It may be a word, phrase, or idea that is being irritatingly overused.

One way to avoid meandering is to build your story methodically, block by block. Be precise in your storytelling. It's almost as if you're telling a story to a little child. In effect you're saying, "And what happened next was . . . And then the next thing was . . . And then . . . And so on, and so on, step by step by step."

Be careful about any of your characters proselytizing. Nothing is more boring than being in an audience and feeling that you're being endlessly lectured or preached at. If you want to get a message across to your audience, be creative; find a way to make it intrinsic to the action of the monologue.

What is the best way to shape and develop your material?

This is where the fine-tuning of the monologue comes in. It requires that you have an overview of the entire piece as well as the ability to pay attention to specific moments and details. It's a constant giving and taking, adding and subtracting, rewriting and refining. Basically it all comes down to your taste and your personal sensibility to the story you're trying to tell.

Too much of this can make it too humorous, too much of that can weigh it down dramatically. Too much exposition here, too much dialogue there. Is that character really necessary? Does he serve any purpose at that point? It goes on and on, questions that only you can pose to yourself and then answer. Be tough on yourself in rewrites.

The Subconscious and Rewrites

Sometimes when working on a piece, writers become frustrated with a problem that they're trying to work out in a particular section. No matter how hard they try, they just can't seem to get it right. Finally, exasperated, they give up on the project for a while, shelve it. This is a good thing to do sometimes, rather than beating your head against a wall.

When the writer returns to the work (with its previously unsolvable problem), he's amazed to find that his creative dilemma is now somehow easily resolved. Having stopped all the efforting and agonizing to make it work, the writer has allowed his subconscious mind to help him out. When you find yourself working too hard on a section for too long, with minimal, diminishing results, perhaps it's time to let it go for a while. Put it in a drawer and just forget about it. When you come back to it with a fresh open mind you may find the problem easily resolved.

COMPLETING WORK ON YOUR MONOLOGUE

The monologue ends when you have completely told the story you set out to tell. Like the opening section, the closing section has a significant effect on an audience. It is the last thing they'll hear from you. Because of their impact, opening and closing sections generally receive the most rewrites in a manuscript.

Things to Keep in Mind in Your Closing

You want to be certain that the closing section has a feeling of completion to it. That doesn't necessarily mean that everything needs to be neatly tied together in the last sentence or two. There are some monologues where the endings seem to just drift off gently. But that lingering element is the exact effect the writer wants to create. It is in keeping with the story that came before it and works organically with the rest of the monologue.

The ending should always be in the same style as the monologue that has preceded it. If you've written a monologue that has a naturalistic feel throughout, you don't want to, in the last line or two, finish it with a bizarre or surreal ending. The jarring quality that an ending like that has will totally confuse and disorient your audience at a very important moment.

You also don't want to end a monologue too abruptly (unless that's in keeping with the monologue's style). If you do, you'll be hearing members of the audience saying, "That's it? It's over? That's the end?" They'll be confused and probably annoyed, and they'll feel cheated that the piece didn't pay off.

And finally, you don't want the ending to go on for too long, having your monologue outstay its welcome. If you dawdle endlessly at the end, you'll notice people in the audience yawning, coughing, and looking at their watches. Say what you have to say, put the period at the end of the sentence, lights down, and then come out for your well-deserved curtain call.

Knowing When the Monologue Is Ready to Be Performed

Only you will know when your monologue is finished. There are several ways to gauge if it still needs some fine-tuning. First, read it as objectively as you can. You should feel absolutely satisfied that you've accomplished everything that you set out to do. Don't be too easy on yourself at this point. Next, if you have yet to locate a director, find one with whom you would want to work, and ask for his comments. (See the sections on selecting and working with a director in the next chapter.) Start performing your monologue as a work in progress for small, select audiences, perhaps in your living room. After each performance, ask the audience members for any comments. If you're hearing the same criticism from several different sources, it might be something that you should look at. Always think of your work as an ongoing process. Even after you've opened and had a run, always look for new things, nuances, moments, etc. Some monologists say that they discover things a year or two later.

A Checklist to Decide if Your Monologue Is Ready to Be Performed

Here are some general points to help you decide if your monologue is complete and ready to be performed. Many of these items have been discussed earlier in the book, but bear repeating at this point.

- Have you told the entire story that you want to tell?
- If you're doing an evening of character monologues, does each one of the individual monologues tell the complete story that you wish to tell?
- When you rehearse the monologue, are there lines of dialogue that feel awkward, unnatural, uncomfortable?
- Do you feel that the characters that you've created are ones that you're able to get inside of? If not, what do you think the problem is? Is it the dialogue, the character, the situation, etc?
- Are there too many characters? Can several similar characters, or characters making the same point, be eliminated?
- Are there too many locations, too many scenes? Will the audience know where they are at any given moment?

- Are there sections that seem to stand out, that don't fit within the shape or form of the rest of the monologue?
- Sometimes an idea in a particular section may work, but the way that your character's expressing it doesn't. Also, you may find that a particular section doesn't have the same style or rhythm as the rest of the piece.
- Are there any sections that could be condensed? Are you embellishing where it's not necessary? Quite often, especially in monologues, less is more. Remember, don't dawdle, make your point, and then move on.
- On the other side of the coin, are you sure you've given your audience enough information? Do they need to know more about a character's background, about some plot point, etc?
- Does the piece work cohesively? Do you see sections that go off on tangents, stray from your central points, etc?
- When you read through the monologue, are you satisfied that you have made all the points (arguments) that you set out to make? (That doesn't mean that you're responsible for resolving them.)
- If you've repeatedly been hearing the same type of comments from your director and audience members, have you been able to make the necessary changes? If you don't agree with their comments, ask yourself why.
- Is there any past-tense dialogue that might be more effective if you brought it into the present?
- Does your piece have a clear beginning, middle, and end?
- Is there an arc, a turning point?

You may have to go through several (or many) drafts of your monologue before you feel that it's ready to be seen by a paying audience.

For those of you who have written short character monologues, the best places to try them out are at acting classes or for friends. I wouldn't recommend trying out new audition material immediately at auditions. Give yourself a few test runs before placing yourself on the line like that. Remember: You won't receive any constructive feedback from the auditioners (even if you do get the job). As to whether you should tell them that you've written the material, that's your call. My experience has been that it's not helpful for them to know, and it can possibly be held against you.

14

PREPARING TO PERFORM

Much of what I'll be discussing here is for those monologists who are looking for a director for their monologue plays. For those of you who would like a director to work with on your shorter, audition monologue, I think you'll still find the following information to be of use. But you should be aware that many directors aren't that interested in working on audition monologues with actors. What you might be looking for are acting coaches who specialize in this type of work.

Selecting a Director

Finding the right director for your piece can be very difficult. Here are some things to consider before committing yourself and your monologue to a particular director. Many monologists find their directors through recommendations from other actors who have worked with them. Another way to select a director is by seeing his work, especially if it's a one-person show. If he has a play in town, try to catch a performance. If you like what you see, give him a call and set up a meeting. If he presently doesn't have any of his work on display, and the recommendation was strong enough, also give him a call. You certainly have nothing to lose.

When meeting with potential directors, always look for directors who are articulate and seem to know what they're talking about. Look for directors who are supportive.

You need to find someone who understands and appreciates your work. Although you certainly don't want a "yes" director, nor do you want to work with someone who is too negative. If, prior to your meeting you've gotten your monologue to him for him to read in advance, ask him to *tell you the story of the monologue as he sees it. Ask him how he sees the piece as a theater piece. Ask him how he likes to work on one-person shows.*

The relationship between monologists and their directors is usually a very intense one. As opposed to a regular play with other actors involved, there's just you and your director. You'll want someone that you feel you can get along with, someone that makes you feel comfortable. If, early into the collaboration, you notice a personality conflict between you and your director (and it can't be worked out), you may want to start looking for a new director as soon as possible.

Working with the Director in Rehearsal

I personally feel that it is always advantageous to rehearse your monologue with a director. Some of you may be planning on directing yourselves. If you honestly feel that you can do it, fine. But remember, having that second set of eyes, that other input, can be very helpful, especially in the pressure-filled final phase of development. If you're determined to direct yourself, at least allow directors that you trust to drop in on occasion and see a rehearsal or two, and get their response.

When you've found a director that you like, you should both set up informal ground rules on how you'd like to work together in rehearsal. You don't want to be too rigid setting up any rules because you'll notice that how you work will evolve as you get to know each other better.

You and your director should both be of the same mind concerning the meaning and interpretation of your piece. You don't have to agree on all aspects of it, but certainly on all the major points. It's sometimes helpful to read through the piece together, then follow with discussion.

Many monologists divide their monologues into small sections, or beats. Slowly and methodically they rehearse each beat. By working this way, two things are accomplished at the same time. First, you'll attain a better understanding of the material you're working on. And second, just by the repetition, you'll learn the text quicker than if you sat down and tried to memorize it by rote.

Once you are in rehearsal, you should be willing to try things that your director suggests, even if they sometimes seem a bit far-fetched. This is a trust issue. You should also feel comfortable enough to fall flat on your face in rehearsal and know that he will still be supportive.

You may notice, from time to time, that you'll be encountering some of the same problems and frustrations that you experienced when you worked on other writer's texts. Even though you wrote the material yourself, you'll come to a word or section that seems difficult to say or realize. It's hard to know what you were originally thinking when you wrote that section, but if you feel it doesn't work now, fix it.

During the rehearsal phase there'll probably be a lot of rewriting. As you become more familiar with the monologue, you'll discover which sections are extraneous to the story you're trying to tell, and which sections still need further development. Because you're working at this point both as an actor and writer, you may at times feel somewhat conflicted. It's at these times that you should rely more on your director's feedback to help with some of the decision making. If your director suggests rewrites on specific sections, listen to what he has to say and feel free to question why he feels any particular rewrite is necessary. Many directors' greatest contribution in the collaboration on your piece will be that as dramaturge. You'll find that some directors can be very helpful with the structuring and order of your piece. If, however, you really feel that a suggestion that they make is not at all what you had in mind, it is your obligation to discuss this with them. Never make any change that you absolutely don't agree with just to appease a director.

It's important that you and your director develop a sincere trust and respect for each other's work during the rehearsal process. Originally, you, the actor-writer, had total control of your project. You must be willing to relinquish some of that power to your director. As you get closer to performance, you may need to rely more heavily on him for his feedback. It's not a time to be questioning his intentions, perceptions, or motives. On the other hand, some actors have a tendency to rely too heavily on their director, making them into a parent figure. Try to maintain your integrity and self-sufficiency, especially when the pressure builds toward performance.

Rehearsing the Audition Monologue

For those of you who are dealing with audition monologues I suggest also rehearsing the piece in beats. Quite often an audition monologue that's rehearsed and memorized by rote sounds it. It may feel a bit strange memorizing your own words, but by and large it's usually easier than memorizing someone else's. And you'll notice that when you audition with your own piece, if you should happen to go up on lines, it's far easier to ad-lib until you come back to the actual text.

Many actors like to use improvisation while rehearsing their audition monologue. Find an improv situation that can connect you to your material. You may notice that when using improvs in rehearsal, new lines of dialogue will come out of your mouth. It's never too late to do rewrites.

One word of caution, don't get too married to your own words. What I mean is: When I used to use some of my own monologues for auditions, there was always a part of me (the writer part) that wanted to make sure that the auditors heard every one of my terrific words. By keeping this as your intention, you can lose the focus of what you're really trying to say in your monologue. They'll hear all your fabulous words, but they won't be getting the deeper meaning, the *character's* intention. In rehearsal try working more with images, thoughts, and intentions, rather than just on memorizing the words themselves.

Performing the Piece

Deciding when the monologue is ready to be performed is a decision that both you and your director should make together. The director can give you a sense of how it looks out there to an audience. And you can let him know how it feels to you, from inside. Many actors at this point are dealing with their nerves and insecurities. Having a director reassure you that the piece is ready can be very helpful at this last phase.

The show will continue to grow after you begin to perform it. Every audience will teach you something about your show. The audience is the last ingredient in the process. Once you start performing the monologue, *everyone* will offer his opinion and comments. Don't allow all these "helpful comments" to sabotage what you and your director have worked out together. Outsiders don't understand the creative process that has gone on during rehearsal. If someone makes a comment that you feel may be useful, mention it to your director; see what he thinks.

Prior to an actual theatrical engagement, it's always smart to have friends and supporters see a few final dress rehearsals before the actual production. Once again, you and your director should agree as to when and if this is necessary.

MARKETING
YOUR SOLO SHOW

O nly you can decide when your mono-
logue(s) is ready for public perfor-
mances. (See "A Checklist to Decide if Your Monologue Is Ready to Be Performed" in
chapter 13.)

If you live in a city that has a small theater where solo material is performed, contact the theater and see if they'll allow you to perform and further develop your piece
in front of an audience. Sometimes theaters allow this on their dark nights. Generally
actors are required to do their own publicity and provide an audience for such performances.

If you do find a theater that will allow you to perform your work, it's in your best
interest to do everything in your power to get literary and/or talent agents to come down
to see the show (see appendix F, Literary Agents). They can be very helpful later on in
moving your piece to other venues.

Another way to promote your work is to send it out to theaters that are looking
for new solo material (see appendix B, Theaters That Accept Solo Material). To save
time and energy *do not* send material to theaters unsolicited, unless they permit it.

There are also contests (see appendix D, Playwriting Competitions That Accept
Solo Material) where you can enter your monologue and perhaps receive a prize and/or
a production to perform your work.

Preparing Your Marketing Package

Your solo-show package should consist of:

- The manuscript of your play
- A videotape of you performing it (if possible)
- A cover letter
- Your résumé
- A synopsis of your monologue

These are only to be sent to theaters, agents, or organizations that accept unsolicited material or that have requested that you send them your material. *Do not send this package unsolicited to anyone else!* You'll be wasting your time and money.

THE MANUSCRIPT

The monologue should be neatly typed on white $8\frac{1}{2}'' \times 11''$ paper. The manuscript should have one and a half spaces between lines. Any stage directions should be indented and single-spaced. Make sure the script is neat looking and well typed with no typos. Remember: This script is your calling card; it represents you. I personally check all the pages of every script I send out. It takes a bit of time, but sometimes the photocopy machines screw up. Sections may be put in the wrong order or, even worse, not copied at all. Make sure the script is well bound with no loose papers. Always make sure the manuscript has a title page that includes the name of your play, your name, address, and phone number (or your agent's). If they request that you send a SASE (self-addressed stamped envelope), please do so, or you can more than likely kiss that material good-bye.

THE VIDEOTAPE OF YOU PERFORMING THE SHOW

If you can arrange to have a professional videotape made of you performing your show, by all means do so. Try to videotape your show in front of a live audience. You'll want a lot of close-ups of you performing the piece on the videotape. You'll also want some shots cutting back and forth from your face to your body. Just so you're forewarned, many of the people to whom you'll be sending your videotapes never return them, so make sure to make multiple copies. Generally, many of the festivals to which you'll be sending the tape want it to be under an hour; try to keep to that rule. Many of the viewers of the videotapes watch about the first five minutes of each tape, so the best advice is to cue the tape up to what you consider a strong section in your show.

YOUR RÉSUMÉ

Your résumé should include all pertinent information such as your name and address, your telephone, fax, and e-mail contact numbers, your theatrical background (including, for example, names of shows and theaters you've performed in), academic and theatrical training that you've had, any theatrical unions that you belong to, and theatrical groups of which you're a member. If your work has been published, make sure to include that on your résumé as well.

I suggest that your résumé should not be your regular acting résumé. It should be a résumé focused more on your one-person show. It should feature any and all information pertaining to your show in strategic areas on the résumé. It should also, however, include all of your other acting credits.

Your Cover Letter

Your cover letter should be addressed to an individual (if possible), rather than to just "literary manager." Let the person know why you are contacting them. Introduce the monologue, and give some basic information about it. Explain why you think your monologue might be right for that specific theater. If you've performed the show at other theaters, include that information. You can mention that the show was well received or if it received good reviews, but don't get into too much detail about it. If you've performed the play in many theaters, there's no reason to list them all, just list the main ones. (The others are listed on your résumé.) Tell the theater a bit about who you are. Let them know that you look forward to hearing from them. If they requested a copy of your monologue prior to this letter, let them know that you're looking forward to hearing from them with their response. End the letter with an expression such as "With warm regards," or "Sincerely."

The Synopsis of Your Monologue

Many writers find it very difficult to summarize the story of their monologue. Unfortunately, in some cases (not too many), the theater or producer requires this summary. Here are some things to keep in mind regarding the synopsis:

Without going into too much detail, briefly summarize the basic features of the plot of your monologue. What is the story you're trying to tell? Your synopsis should include a basic description of the theme and the style of the monologue. Avoid clichéd statements to describe any aspect of the work. Be original, honest, and personal in describing your work. Your synopsis should be a page or less.

Management/Booking Agencies
That Handle Solo Artists

The following are just a few management/booking agencies that work with solo artists. This list is just a starting point; there are many others.

- WASHINGTON SQUARE ARTS
12 East 10th Street
New York, New York 10003
Tel. (212) 253-0333   FAX (212) 253- 0333
E-mail: *krusso@washingtonsquarearts.com*
        mshimkin@washingtonsquarearts.com
Web site: *www.washingtonsquarearts.com*
Contact: Kathleen Russo
   This agency is dedicated to artists who are "unique, challenging, powerful, and fun, artists whose work is designed for diverse and wide ranging audiences." They are a relatively small agency handling a select, hand-picked group of artists. Their present roster includes: Spalding Gray, Danny Hoch, Hazelle Goodman, Holly Hughes, Marga Gomez, Bob Holman, and others.

- COLUMBIA ARTISTS MANAGEMENT, INC. (CAMI)
165 West 57th Street
New York, New York 10019
Tel. (212) 841- 9500
   This company was formed in 1930 when Arthur Judson, a co-founder of the Columbia Broadcast System, merged seven independent concert managers to pool their musical knowledge, commercial know-how and booking facilities. The Corporation consisted of managers whose lists represented the most famous artists of the day and whose activities covered all of North America. Today, aside from solo artists, they also handle ensembles, orchestras, dance companies, and popular and theatrical attractions.
   CAMI is a diversified artist management company offering personal direction for solo artists and performing arts organizations. The company has taken a strong role in finding and developing the careers of solo artists. They handle many solo artists.

- CSTAR (COLUMBIA STAGE ARTISTS MANAGEMENT)
89 Melville Avenue
San Anselmo, CA 94960
Tel. (415) 458-2882   FAX (415) 458-2992
E-mail: *greg@cstartists.com*
Web site: *www.cstartists.com*
Contact: Greg Phillips or Cathy Pruzan
   This relatively small management company handles a select group of artists. Some of their clientele include Kate Clinton, Sherry Glaser, Debby Gravite, and the New Century Chamber Orchestra.

16

Interviews with Monologue Writers and Performance Artists

These were the general questions asked to all of the following artists:

- What prompted you to start writing your own show?
- How and when did you first start?
- Did you have any specific goals, things that you wanted to say, or did you just allow yourself to explore freely?
- How did you begin working? What kinds of things did you do those first times?
- As you developed your piece, how did you shape it or do rewrites to illuminate things?
- How did you deal with self-censoring, doubts, etc.?
- How did you know when the piece was ready?
- How did you rehearse the piece?
- Describe your relationship with your director. Where was he most helpful?
- What was it like performing the piece that first time up? How do you feel the performances have changed?
- What's it like for you to perform your own work every night in front of an audience?
- As you've worked on new material, how would you say your work process has changed?
- What advice do you have for other actors just starting out who want to develop their own one-person shows?

Photo by Paula Cort

SPALDING GRAY

Spalding Gray has created fifteen monologues, which have been performed
throughout the United States, Europe,
and Australia, including *Sex and Death
to the Age 14; Booze, Cars and College
Girls; A Personal History of the American
Theater; India and After (America);
Monster In The Box; Gray's Anatomy;*
and *Swimming to Cambodia.* Appear-
ances on and off-Broadway include the
portrayal of the stage manager in *Our
Town,* directed by Gregory Mosher, and
the Performance Group's New York premiere of Shepard's *Tooth of Crime.* He
co-founded the Wooster Group, and he wrote and performed the autobiographical
trilogy, *Three Places in Rhode Island.* Film credits include Roland Joffe's *The Killing
Fields,* Jonathan Demme's *Swimming to Cambodia,* David Byrne's *True Stories, Clara's
Heart, Beaches,* and *The Paper.* Publications include a collection of monologues, *Sex
and Death to the Age 14* (Random House), *Swimming to Cambodia* (Theater Communications Group), *In Search of the Monkey Girl* (Aperure Press), *Gray's Anatomy* (Vintage),
and the novel *Impossible Vacation* (Knopf). *It's a Slippery Slope* was published by Fer-
rar, Strauss, and Giroux, and was released on compact disc (Mercury Records). Mr.
Gray has received a Guggenheim Fellowship and grants from the National Endowment
for the Arts and The Rockefeller Foundation. His *Swimming to Cambodia* won the
Obie Award.

- Peter Marks, in the *New York Times,* called Gray "the grand master of the first
  person singular . . . " and went on to say, "*It's a Slippery Slope* is a clear eyed
  and life-affirming performance piece."
- Writing of *It's a Slippery Slope,* Mark Wasburn of the *Village Voice* wrote,
  "Spalding Gray's brilliant life-monologue is in another league. Funny and touching, Gray slides down the slopes of his uncertainties, creating a theatrical landscape of remarkable internal dimension."

Interview with Spalding Gray

STARTING OUT

First of all it's important to say that I don't start off writing material, although I like to
consider myself a writer. I'm definitely an aural composer.

I was working with the Wooster Group in 1976 and 1977; I was evolving with the group theater pieces that involved stories of my life. One of the seminal pieces was *Rumstick Road,* which was about my mother's suicide. In that I'd do little direct addresses to the audience. I'd be saying, "This is me, I'm Spalding Gray, and this is what happened to me." Those little stories, when printed up, read like writing. I saw that I was doing a form of autobiographic writing. But it was theatricalized, made into theatrical metaphors by Elizabeth LeCompte (the director).

Going Solo (How I Work)

Once I split from the Wooster Group (1979), I wanted to go solo. But what I wanted to do was tell my story. So I sat at a little desk in the Performing Garage in September of 1979 and started telling my story, beginning with the first monologue, *Sex and Death at the Age 14* (later performed at the Performing Garage).

I sat down with an outline to guide me through the narrative of memories, but then I tape-recorded it and listened to what I had said. It was that way of working that gave me my structure. The next evening I went back after listening to it and tied it all together. So in that sense you might say I was working structurally from the original memory. I wasn't sitting down and saying, "How would this go better?" If I had any goals in mind, it was just to tell the audience the stories, my stories. I'd see how it sat with the audience.

I don't like to rehearse. My first rehearsal is with and in front of an audience. I say that I work improvisationally, but the way it's different from most improv people is that eventually I want it to be set. Most improv people want it to stay open and keep on opening up. When I was a traditional actor I had to memorize lines and then pretend that I didn't know them. Now I don't memorize lines because there are no lines. It's like bushwhacking.

In a way I'm corralling memories and trying to find the right words for them each time. And that's what gives it its freshness. And that's what makes the audience think that I'm saying it for the first time. Because what they're witnessing is something that's in the moment. And what that is is a recollection each evening of a text that is only in the memory.

Rewriting

The way I rewrite is by doing the next performance. So, in a sense, I get paid to rewrite. I tape each performance for sometimes up to thirty shows. Each tape is new and helpful, filled with insights. I think better in front of an audience. Between the first show and the thirtieth show I believe the detail of the story changes, as does the structure.

As the shows progress I get more cinemagraphic and do quicker cuts. I have a photographic memory, and at the beginning I tend to remember too much, there's just too much information. It's like a kid telling his dream. As I go along I cut to the chase and get better and better. As far as clarity, let's think about water going down a mountain.

It runs all different trails until it finds that one trail. In my work, once it finds that one trail, the piece suddenly becomes clearer, a condensed stream of thought. But that one comes through many flows, believe me. That's what it is for me. It takes many performances to lead to that absolute heightened language that is no longer just chatting to the audience. So when I sit down and perform my *It's a Slippery Slope* piece, which I really know, having performed it for four years, I can go right into it. I immediately find all the rhythms.

I think each piece goes through at least three clear delineations. The first is the actual public memory with the audience, where I'm speaking it and trying to figure it out for myself with them. My early audiences get to see me discovering things. I'm doing it with them. There's an enormous amount of dialogue there at the beginning.

The audience began, quite a while ago, to teach me and give me my sense of humor. I've developed it with them. I had been more of an existentially dark, tortured, New Englander. I think by coming to New York, I came to the right place to find dialectic. I really think of my work as a dialogue with the audience.

MY SENSE OF REALITY

I remember when I was an actor playing roles, I always felt a bit removed. I would think things like, "This isn't really me. This isn't really real, and this didn't really happen." I've personally always felt that life is such a dream, such a fiction, so ephemeral. It only comes around once. It has no thing to compare it to. So I think that my monologues are a form of coming 'round twice. First of all, reincarnation, by retelling the story. And also of grounding myself, by saying, "I'm Spalding Gray and this happened to me."

I don't make up fictitious stories; it's not my way of working. My son Forrest, who is now five, will sometimes ask me to tell him a scary story. And nothing ever comes to mind, no story. And finally exhausted, I'll say "Forrest, this is the scary story; just look around."

SELF-CENSORS

When my self-censors come in, which only occurs minimally, I welcome them. Otherwise, I tend to get too self-indulgent. By the way, my definition of self-indulgence is lack of awareness.

What is narcissism? A narcissist is someone who doesn't know he's a narcissist. As long as I'm aware (through hearing the tape) of what I'm saying, then I can at least make conscious choices and accept it or not accept it.

STORYTELLING

I'm always testing out my stories on the people that I live with because I'm a storyteller. I'll start talking at the end of the day, incessantly. I make outline journals in my head of, say, some thing or things that happened yesterday. And then I'll tell the stories to Kathy (the woman I live with), or my therapist, or whomever. I'll say certain keywords that remind me of the event. At some point in my process of developing a piece, I'll call in what I call a creative consultant, to help me, just be a mirror to what I'm saying. I'll say to him, "Here's what I'm hearing. What could go better?"

What I do with an audience is transference. That's where the dance is, where the dialogue is, where they affect me. A year or so after performing a piece I will call a director in because sometimes the piece has become unwieldy or too long. It can use some minor tuning. When we did the CD of *It's a Slippery Slope,* James Taylor was the producer. It was James's ears and fresh take on the material that enabled me to go through the whole process of recording it. He was hearing it fresh and was excited by it.

Photo by Ron Rinaldi

MARY LOUISE WILSON

Ms. Wilson's one-woman show, *Full Gallop,* was performed at the Bay Street Theater, The Manhattan Theater Club, and at the Westside Arts Theater off-Broadway. Most recently she performed the play in London. On Broadway she has appeared in *Showboat* (Harold Prince, director), *Prelude to a Kiss* (Norman Rene, director), Neil Simon's *Fools* (Mike Nichols, director), *Alice in Wonderland* (Eva LaGallienne, director), *The Philadelphia Story* (Ellis Rabb, director), *Gypsy* (Arthur Laurents, director), and *The Royal Family.* Off-Broadway, she appeared in *Baby with the Bathwater* (Playwrights Horizons, Jerry Zaks, director), *Sister Mary Ignasius Explains It All for You* (Playwrights Horizons, Jerry Zaks, director), and *Buried Child* (Theater Dy Lys, Robert Woodruff, director). She has worked in film with directors such as Woody Allen (*Zelig*), Alan J. Pakula (*Klute*), Susan Seidleman (*She Devil*), Per Weir (*Green Card*), Chris Columbus (*Stepmom*), and Collin Higgins (*Best Little Whorehouse in Texas*). *Full Gallop* won the Drama Desk award, the Obie Award, and received an Outer Critics Circle Nomination. Her performance in *Cabaret* (1998 Broadway revival) garnered her a Tony nomination.

- Vincent Canby, in his *New York Times* review of *Full Gallop,* wrote, "In addition to Vreeland's invigorating buccaneer personality, *Full Gallop* calls attention to the evolution of the one-character play as an unexpectedly rewarding, freewheeling source of entertainment in the contemporary theater. . . . [T]he play effortlessly unfolds as a high-flying, idiosyncratic memoir, a history of a marriage, a family and a gaudy career."

Interview with Mary Louise Wilson

INSPIRATION

When I was a child I was fascinated with Ruth Draper, so I thought about monologues, but it didn't seem like something someone did in modern times. I hated the idea of a one-woman show. A one-person show just seemed like something that couldn't be done. You needed two actors for a play to happen. The only one-woman show that I ever saw that I liked was Pat Carroll's *Gertrude Stein*. I liked that show very much, was very impressed with it. It was an inspiration to me.

MY DECISION

To be honest with you, I decided to do my show because I was so fed up with where I was in the business, the work I was getting. I thought, "What the hell have I got to lose?" I'd spent years playing nurses and maids and secretaries, really boring and unnourishing stuff.

A friend of mine, Mark Hampton (co-writer), was as fascinated as I was with Diana Vreeland. When she died I realized that I must get the rights to the book *D.V.* I thought if I don't get the rights to it someone else will and then I'd kick myself for the rest of my life. I was amazed that they actually entertained the idea of Mark and I possibly doing this. It seemed that each step of the way the door would actually open.

MY FASCINATION

I've always been fascinated by people in power and what happens to them when they lose their power. Also, I understand what it's like to be out of work. But mostly, the woman (Vreeland) is so different from me. She was such an up, such a survivor. She had a joy in living that was pretty irresistible. She was a combination of what I always wanted to be as a kid, funny and glamorous at the same time. I remember as a child thinking that Carmen Miranda was someone else "who had it."

STARTING OUT

Mark and I sat around for days, talking and taking notes. Then we took the book *D.V.* and indexed it into sections. We whittled it down to our favorite stories. We also had access to audiotapes of her talking, so we also had the advantage of learning how she told a story. We also read other things about her, what other people said, interviews, etc. At first she was hilarious, just that; then we began to find her very moving. I found her gallant, no bitchiness about her, not interested in going on about something she hated.

Getting back to those first steps, I filled legal pads with notes that we took from all our research. There were index cards that had various stories laid out. We played with the arrangement of things. We were trying to build it, give it a climax. We decided to only use stories that were germane to moving the play forward. It really was heart-breaking, because there were a lot of great stories that we couldn't use.

MAKING CHOICES

As far as shaping the piece, I used *Gertrude Stein* as a model. The things that were most important to me were the following questions:

1. Where are we?
2. Who are we?
3. Who are we talking to?
4. Where is the character in her life?

Answering those questions is, I believe, crucial to a successful one-person show. I find so often they are not addressed in one-person shows. I spent months answering them.

So what we had were these wonderful stories. What we needed was a linkage, something that could hold them together. Basically what we needed to supply now was a dramatic line.

Originally we had a maid in the piece, another character. She would come on and say, "Oui" or "No." We thought this was great. But eventually, as the piece developed, we let her go. You must realize that we took six years to write the play. We did readings and workshops during that time. And after each reading or workshop we would take another leap forward in the development of the script.

COLLABORATION

Since this was collaboration, you should understand the relationship that I had with my co-writer, Mark Hampton. We both intuitively understood the woman. But I, as an actor, was trying to make everything real and not campy, based in emotional things. Mark wanted to put in jokes. We both would give into each other depending on how it went in the reading.

From the very beginning I knew that there had to be one set, and it had to be where she would talk. It seemed inevitable that it should be her living room.

WORKSHOPS

The readings would be done all over. Once we did one at Playwrights Horizons, and Andre Bishop invited us to do a reading at a ladies club. At that reading we met Sybil Burton. She arranged for us to do full-out productions for two weekends at Bay Street (in Sag Harbor). We did readings at Julliard (a fundraiser), at nightclubs, wherever. After one reading, in this nightclub, a friend of mine saw it and mentioned it the next day to Jack O'Brien. It was at that nightclub fundraiser that we got a director and a literary agent.

DEVELOPMENT

I took on her manner and voice in rehearsals. I'd walk on the road near where I live in the country, and memorize it. Mark would be my outside eye. We continued to rewrite even after we did it at the Old Globe, right up until we opened at the Manhattan Theater Club. One of the lessons that I learned while working on her was to intuit the way she would say things.

When the director came into the picture the whole piece took on more of a physical life. Mark stopped coming to rehearsals after the piece was finally down on paper. The director took over at that point.

I did find it somewhat difficult going from being the writer to just being the actor. I remember time and again, looking at a line and saying, "Who wrote this? I can't say this!" It was a bit conflicting.

A LESSON LEARNED

In order to write what you want to say you have to write badly. It's the biggest lesson that I've learned. Say, I wanted Diana to be really witty. I'd write the first thing that comes into my head. Quite often it will be terrible the first time. That wouldn't be discouraging, it just meant I'd have to improve on what I just wrote. You have to learn to say, "No, that isn't what I want to say. This is what I want to say!" When you're stuck you can't wait for inspiration, you just have to sit down and write!

FULL GALLOP

We got the name *Full Gallop* after a lunch that I had with Vreeland's son (I had to be approved of). He told me that she always had visitors over, even when she was ill. If she didn't feel well enough to come out of her bedroom, the maid would serve the guests a meal, and they would talk to her through the door. He said, "Mom never liked to appear unless she was at full gallop."

WRITING WITH A PARTNER

I think that it's great to work with someone; it's a huge help. When the two of you show up, then you have to do something. There is the responsibility to your partner. There were, however, days of staring contests, where nothing happened. It would be terrible. Fortunately they were rare. Also, working with someone may not be for everyone. It really is a marriage.

OTHER THINGS THAT I'VE LEARNED

One thing I'd like to go back to is working on index cards. I found them a very valuable tool. The cards can be placed on the floor and can assist you in finding the play's arc.

You can rearrange them over and over until you have the best sequence, the best arrangement.

Something else that fascinated me while working on this piece was the amount of minutiae that you unearth about a person's life. I would explore how she would get ready in the morning, the objects she touched, her life.

A Last Thought

Another piece of advice: You have to connect with the audience. It's imperative in this type of theater. You must feel them and be open to them. In a sense they are your scene partner. I have found that doing a one-person play is very empowering for actors. I hope that other actors don't wait as long as I did to get started. There is so much pleasure in this type of theater.

Helen K. Garber copyright 1999

CHARLAYNE WOODARD

Charlayne Woodard's first play, *Pretty Fire*, which she wrote and performed, enjoyed successful engagements at the Manhattan Theater Club and at Seattle Repertory Company. It was published by Penguin Press. Her second play, *Neat*, also enjoyed sold-out runs at the Manhattan Theater Club, Seattle Repertory Theater, and The Mark Taper Forum in Los Angeles. As an actress, Ms. Woodard performed in the original cast of *Ain't Misbehavin'* on Broadway. Off-Broadway she performed in such shows as *Hang On to the Good Times* at the Manhattan Theater Club, George C. Wolfe's production of *The Caucasian Chalk Circle,* and opposite Michelle Pfeiffer in *Twelfth Night* at The New York Shakespeare Festival. Regionally she has worked at the LaJolla Playhouse in Tony Kushner's adaptation of *The Good Person of Setzuan* (with Lou Diamond Phillips). Film credits include: *The Crucible* with Winona Ryder, John Schlesinger's *Eye for an Eye*, with Sally Field, and in *One Good Cop* with Michael Keaton. Television credits include: *Run for the Dream, The Gail Dever's Story* (playing Gail Dever), Oprah Winfrey's *The Wedding,* and *Buffalo Girls* with Melanie Huston and Angelica Huston. *Pretty Fire* won a Los Angeles Drama Critics Award and the NAACP Theater award for Best Play and Best Playwright. *Neat* was nominated for an Outer Critics Circle Award and an Ovation Award (Los Angeles) for Best Play and Best Actress. It won the prestigious Irving and Blache Laurie Theater Vision Award. Acting awards include: Tony and Drama desk nominations for *Ain't Misbehavin,* a second Drama Desk nomination for *Hang On to the Good Times.* Ms. Woodard received an AUDELCO nomination for her performance in George C. Wolfe's production of *The Caucasian Chalk Circle.*

- David Richard, in the *New York Times,* called *Pretty Fire* "one of the most positive pictures of the Black-American experience I've seen on stage."
- Howard Waxman, in *Variety,* said of her second play, *Neat,* . . . "a frequently funny, often frightening and ultimately very moving series of vignettes. . . . With just a few carefully nuanced gestures and vocal changes, Ms. Woodard offers a spectacular gallery of family portraits."

Interview with Charlayne Woodard

STARTING OUT

I had moved to Los Angeles. I believe that if I'd stayed in New York, I'd never have written anything. I was too busy working all the time. When I moved to L.A., I thought I'd be just as busy tackling new stuff. That's not how it worked out though. I was getting guest spots on TV shows with like three lines or something. And even though I'd be on the set all week, I had a lot more time. Between guest-spot gigs you might have like two weeks of nothing. And I was so used to working. So I'd come back home just to do a play. I kept feeling I've got to keep my chops, I've got to keep my chops.

So I decided, since I'm a member of the Actors Studio, to work on a piece. I wanted to work on something just for myself. I felt if I kept working on something, that would keep my chops up. At the same time, I was meeting with lots of people, and I'm talking a lot, because basically I'm a storyteller. I found myself telling people about my life. People out here in L.A., it seemed to me, had never met anyone like me. In some sense L.A. is a very segregated town. I felt that I had to explain myself when I was around people who weren't black. I'd tell them about where I came from, my family, like that.

THE PEOPLE WHO PROMPTED ME TO WRITE

I had this friend Shirley who's an artist. And she said she hadn't had a black model in over fifty years. She asked me if I'd sit for her. Now what can you say to that? Of course, I said yes. So as I sat there posing for her, I told her about my life. And she said, "You must write this down." My husband had also been prompting me to write my stories down. But, prior to this time in L.A., I never had time. I was reluctant to start writing. I thought I was an actor only.

Cut to: My bishop's wife had asked me to sing at this women's retreat. I said, "No way." I mean everyone there sings like Jennifer Holiday. She said, "Look, I'll give you twenty minutes to do anything you want. It doesn't have to be singing." That's when I wrote my first story. It was about what turned me into being an actor. It's called "Joy." It's the last piece of my first show, *Pretty Fire*.

HOW I WORK

My process is to talk. I must have a person to talk to. I'd been telling the story of "Joy" for a year. Many of the stories in *Pretty Fire*, I'd been telling around for over a year. At dinner parties, lunches, wherever. When you have a person listening to your stories, you can see their reactions immediately. If they look confused, you realize you have to clarify. Next time you tell that same story, you won't have that same confused moment. . . . People's emotional reactions are very helpful to me. When they say, "Oh my God, I'm having goosebumps!" Or, "Oh my God I'm crying," I know I've hit a nerve.

Then I'll tell that same story three or four more times over maybe a year. Then I'll write it down. I'm constantly refining it. When I finally get to the point where I write the thing down, that's basically what you're going to see.

I start off with a script that's really fat; then slowly I begin making cuts. I don't just want a lot of monologues; I want a night of theater. It's after I'm on my feet with the piece that I start really rewriting, living the piece. Basically I create from the doing. Once you are on your feet, you no longer tell your story; you start to live it. You'll find that you can cut a lot of expositional material now because you're doing them.

I live every minute, sensorially. In my plays sensory things are everywhere just so I can hook in. The sensory informs my emotions. That's what makes it exciting for me. I try to tell as little of the story as possible. My rehearsal period is about: How can I stop just telling this, and show it?

In *Neat*, I talk about how my aunt had an epileptic seizure. And I wrote a beautiful thing about how she jerked around and how her body followed, and how she banged into a chinaberry tree, bounced around, etc. In rehearsal, I decided to try actually doing it rather than just talking about it. It really upset me. But that was a good thing. I said, okay that's real, we keep it.

I was doing *Pretty Fire* in Seattle. During a break, I told Dan Sullivan a story about my aunt. He loved the story and said, "Charlayne, create a play about it and we'll workshop next year." So for a whole year I told stories about that phase of my life. Then we workshopped the piece at Seattle.

REHEARSING WITH A DIRECTOR

The way I rehearse is, I enter the room; the director's there; and I stand up and just start reading what I wrote, just like that. It's usually kind of not happening at that moment. It feels stilted. I change the words as I talk in rehearsal. Then I start moving around, writing down the changes. The director will remember the stuff that you came up with.

The script is just an outline with the main points. Sometimes I go off to a whole other thing that I'm reminded of, and then that new thing becomes part of the play. My workshop process is where I actually write it.

MY AUDIENCE AND MY ANCHORS

A play is not complete until I have the workshop audience. They tell me what is and isn't working. They are my scene partners. I never feel alone on the stage except for the first ten seconds. It's at that point that I look out and see what I call "my anchors." I find two anchors out in the audience, two people who are just waiting and ready. I start off just telling those two people my story. Then I open it up to the whole audience. My intention is, "Let me tell you something." Pretty soon the whole stage gets crowded with all my characters. I don't feel alone anymore. All of their reactions make you feel good, goose you.

HOW THE PIECE EVOLVES

In the workshop production I read the play off the page. When I'm in an actual production I have the piece in my soul. Ideally, by the last performance of a run I'm living and breathing every minute of it. I let it take me on a ride. Early on (in workshop and early previews), you can't expect to be taken on a ride. It feels strange and it can sometimes be difficult. All through previews I'm constantly changing it. You just have to roll with it through those tough times. The way it finally becomes part of your soul is when you've connected with audiences. Once we open, however, I freeze the show. But I don't ever freeze my life in it.

Copyright Dona Ann McAdams

DANNY HOCH

Danny Hoch performed his solo show *Some People* at P.S. 122 and at the Joseph Papp Public Theater in 1994 (directed by Jo Bonney). The show toured over twenty U.S. cities as well as Austria, Cuba, and Scotland. It also aired on HBO. Danny has written and acted for television and several films including HBO's *Subway Stories*, Terrence Malick's *Thin Red Line*, and Fox Searchlight's *Whiteboys*. His writings have appeared in *Harper's* and *New Theater Review*. *Out of Character; Jails, Hospitals and Hip-Hop;* and *Some People* were recently published by Villard Books, a division of Random House. *Jails, Hospitals and Hip-Hop* is being made into a film and a spoken word CD; it is on a forty-city tour through the millennium. Danny won an Obie and a Fringe First Award (Edinburgh Festival) for his solo show *Some*

People. The show was nominated for a Cable Ace Award for the HBO production. He is the recipient of a Solo Theater Fellowship from the National Endowment for the Arts, a Sundance Writers Fellow, a CalArts/Alpert Award, and a Tennessee Williams Fellow. At Berkeley Repertory Theater, *Jails . . .* received a Bay Area theater Critics Circle Award for Outstanding Solo Performance and a Drama Desk Award Nomination.

- The *New York Times* called Hoch "a remarkable young performer who finds crusted layers of cultural contradictions . . . part sociologist, part moralist, and part super-chameleon."
- James Hannaham, in the *Village Voice,* said, "[Hoch's] characters are beautifully developed, in an honest and virtuosic style. . . . [His] strength lies in his ability to represent people as they are rather than as political discourse would dictate."

Interview with Danny Hoch

I Never Wanted to Be a Writer

I never wanted to be a writer; I only wanted to act. But there was no theater, film, or TV that reflected my generation or responded to my community. So why be an actor if you're going to act about nothing that has to do with your community? I developed my work, orally, in front of an audience. I've forced myself to become a writer, but that's certainly not how it started out.

My first show was a piece called *Pot Melting,* at a place called the Gas Station on the lower east side. It was about ninety minutes long.

My Background

I had graduated from Performing Arts High School and went on to North Carolina School for the Arts. I ultimately dropped out because the goal was to go back to New York after four years and audition for the same agents, casting directors, and producers that I had auditioned for when I was at Performing Arts. I stopped looking through *Backstage* and returning calls from the agents who were calling me for work that I just couldn't relate to, or didn't connect to. The material that was around just seemed ridiculous to me.

Getting Started

So I just started creating these monologues. I did them in front of audiences that I had invited either to my house, or at some performance evening somewhere. I'd work on ten or twenty minutes worth of new material, and just start riffing, in character, in front of the audience. I knew who the characters were, where they were, and why they were there. But the dialogue, the language could go anywhere, anyplace. The goal was to let the characters live and breathe. Eventually, after doing the characters many times, I got rid of what didn't work, kept what did. I worked totally from memory.

MY FIRST SHOW

Eventually I had ninety minutes and about fourteen characters (two were eventually cut out). Initially I had a four-night run at the Gas Station, but that short run turned into a four-month run, based on pure word of mouth.

Later, as I toured the show, the characters kept evolving. They were living, breathing characters, not confined to a page. As time went on and issues changed, so did the characters. I worked mostly on structure and improvisation. I guess you can say that's how I work. Some characters, in subsequent shows, were offshoots of those original characters.

SOME PEOPLE

My next show, *Some People,* evolved a lot because I toured with it and did it so often. It was constantly changing. For instance, there was one character whose dialogue had completely changed from when I first did him, totally! I mean he was talking about totally different things because time had changed.

JO BONNEY

By the time I got to the Public Theater I was writing things down, because I was working with a director, Jo Bonney. She forced me to write down everything I was saying. Initially, I was very reluctant because I thought we're getting into literary dramatics here, and I don't want to be a playwright. I told her, "I don't write stories. I work with pure characters and oral language." It's the most organic and visceral way for me to work. If I'm sitting in front of a computer and trying to write dialogue, it's very un-organic for me. I'd feel detached, very intellectual, working like that. But Jo said, "If you look at what you've said, on the page, you'll be able to dramaturge your own work, and see what the flow of it is."

See, when I'm onstage, I'm in a relationship with the audience. It's just them and me. So at those times, obviously, it's impossible for me to have a third eye. That's the work of the director, to be that third eye.

WHAT I'M TRYING TO SAY (PERSONAL GOALS)

The goal, for me, is the telling of the story. In the United States, most of us are not indigenous to this place. We come from many cultures and histories and languages. The idea that we're supposed to get along and understand each other is preposterous. The idea of one government and one president just doesn't make sense to me. So how do we wind up communicating? How do we communicate across cultures that claim us, even though we don't belong to it?

Everything is language. My mother is a speech pathologist, constantly working with all sorts of speech problems. As a kid I was a mime. Actually, I was a street mime for many years. I think it's a combination of the knowledge I have of my mother's work and my mime experience that informed a lot of what I do.

THE ROLE OF THE DIRECTOR

Some of my characters took three years to evolve; some took just four days. I think Jo Bonney was a major catalyst to my work. She brought in a critical development. What she brought was an understanding of the dramatic experience. I was coming from a place that was way inside the character.

As an actor I was concerned with what the audience was thinking at different times. As a playwright, however, I could have cared less. I wasn't concerned about having a story with a through-line. My only concern was: Is this character living and breathing? Jo Bonney came into the picture as a dramaturge-director.

To me theater must be functional. Theater, for me, must be the most powerful form of communication; otherwise it's not functional.

I used to create with wild abandon, until there were critical eyes on me, then I thought about self-censoring. But really I think I still walk the edge.

I think a piece is never really finished; it's always ongoing. I notice that the longer I work on a show, tour with it, etc., the more it seems to evolve.

MY BEST MONOLOGUE

It's interesting that one of the best monologues I have is one that I wrote first, something, as I said, I never do. It's a wonderful piece. Ironically, when I got up to perform it, I didn't do it. I mean I couldn't physically perform it in front of the audience. When Jo asked me why I couldn't do it, I told her, it's because I wrote it first. The difference was that there was a story I wanted to tell, rather than a voice that I wanted to hear.

LESSONS LEARNED

The important questions to keep in mind when writing solo shows are: What is the drama? What is universal about your show? It's not enough for an actor to get up on a stage and tell his life story.

I don't rehearse like most actors do. When I meet with Jo, we do a lot of sitting and talking. The majority of our rehearsal time is dramaturging, not physically rehearsing. We practically wait until tech before deciding if I'll go, say, to stage left or right to do a moment. The real rehearsing is in front of an audience.

THE AUDIENCE

My sense of performing in front of an audience is, on the one hand, it's lonely because you're the only one up there. There's no one else to share the energy with. On the other level, it is very fulfilling because you're sharing that energy with the audience, and you don't have to share it with anybody else.

Every audience is different, depending on who's dominating the audience. If the audience is dominated by *New York Times*–reading people from the suburbs, I don't feel so great. Many of these people are coming purely to be just entertained. There's a sense that they deserve to be there more than other people. And we get into this deservement kind of thing. You know, I deserve to be here, I paid for my ticket type situation. When I'm in a university theater situation, say in Kansas, chances are my show will be a lot better.

JUST ASK YOURSELF

I constantly ask people who want to do solo shows, "Who is your audience, and who do you want your audience to be?" My personal dream audience is between sixteen and twenty-five years old, and diverse economically, racially, linguistically.

MY PROCESS THEN AND NOW

My process really hasn't changed much since I started. It's really only accelerated and has become fine-tuned. I do however, write things down now. I work in front of an audience, do my shows, and then write it down, rather than just remembering it from show to show. But I don't actually put it on paper until after doing it maybe eight or ten times in front of the audience. I don't write it down to memorize it. That's not the purpose. I rarely even look at it. I give it to Jo, and she discusses it dramaturgically with me. Then I try to remember the structural changes.

THE THING TO KEEP IN MIND

The important thing for your readers to ask themselves is, "What is your purpose in doing a one-person show?" If it's just for commercial success, you'll find yourself very disappointed, especially after putting all that work into the show. I've seen it happen to a dozen people.

Photo by Alan Kirschen

DAEL ORLANDERSMITH

Dael has toured extensively with the Nuyorican Poet's Café throughout the United States, Europe, and Australia. She has appeared in productions of *Macbeth, Romeo and Juliet,* and *A Raisin in the Sun.* She can be seen in an offbeat role in Hal Hartley's *Amateur.* She premiered her one-person show *Monster* at the prestigious New York Theater Workshop as part of the Solo Mio festival. Her solo show *The Gimmick* was performed as a work in progress at the Sundance Film Festival.

It later ran as a commissioned work by the McCarter Theater and then at The Long Wharf theater and at The New York Theater Workshop. Other solo pieces are *Liar, Liar* (American Place Theater) and *Leftover Life to Kill* (MCC Theater). Dael won an Obie Award for her solo show *Beauty's Daughter.*

- Peter Marks, in the *New York Times,* said, "*Monster* is a courageous performance piece. . . . There is no hint of pretension, not the slightest trace of sentimentality, in [Orlandersmith's] funny, dead-on impressions of her relatives, friends and neighbors. . . . "
- Wilborn Hampton, in the *New York Times,* said of *Beauty's Daughter:* "First and foremost, Ms. Orlandersmith is a poet possessed of an exciting new voice. . . . The language of Ms. Orlandersmith's poetry is like an electric charge, living in imagination and illuminating in its insights, at once full of anger and compassion."

Interview with Dael Orlandersmith

Why I Started

I began to do this, quite frankly, because there wasn't any work for me as a black actor. When I walked in to audition, they'd say things like either gain fifty pounds or lose fifty pounds, or go get your jaw broken or something. They were not very encouraging with accepting me the way I was.

It seems like as black women, we graduated from playing heroin prostitutes to crack head prostitutes, or playing welfare mothers. The opposite end of that was total conservative stuff like *The Cosby Show.* I didn't fit into any of those molds. I'd think, "I'm an actor, I can do all kinds of work. Just give me a chance." But no one was giving me the work. The kind of things people would say was, "I can't wait for the day where everybody could do every role, regardless of color." Those were what I called "POPs," people of power. They're the ones who could do this, they have the ducats. But they were waiting for someone else to do it; then they'd just jump on the bandwagon. So I was being stereotyped left, right, and center. Obviously I got pretty disgusted with the way things were.

When I'd look for monologues, the only things that appealed to me were things like from *Colored Girls,* or *A Raisin in the Sun,* stuff like that. So I began to write my own stuff back in like '87–88. I got accepted into the Actors Studio by contacting Estelle Parsons, letting her see my work. She said, "You should be writing every day." It was then, at that time, that the writing really began to happen.

Important Influences

My favorite playwright is Eugene O'Neill; my favorite poet is Rimbaud. I'm heavily influenced by like poetry and stuff. I loved Rimbaud's process of the disorganization of the senses. I wanted to do that with language. I wanted to attack the senses, and show and delineate the human condition, no matter how dark it is. I want to bring it to a light. And that's what I think that people like Eugene O'Neill and Rimbaud do, they show us the darkness, the morbidness of the human condition. Because we all have it. It's what's hidden, what we hide. It's the thing that makes us afraid. I like the kind of theater that keeps me on a certain edge, forces me to look in myself in certain ways, forces me to think.

How I Feel about Things

I was talking about this piece I'm writing, and this guy said, "Your piece bothered me because there was no redemption, no hope." I told him I wasn't interested in redemption or hope just for the sake of redemption or hope. I'm interested in what is real. The truth is that sometimes some people just don't make it. It's very easy to sugar coat something. But the truth of the matter is in some situations there's just no hope. I'm not writing the way I do just so that people will perceive my work as morbid, or dark, or deep. It's just what interests me.

My favorite painter is Francis Bacon. My thing is, what we perceive as normal is false. The nine to five thing, the coffee break, hour off for lunch thing is a joke. The average life span is seventy-five. You do this until you're sixty-five years old and then wonder, "How come I'm not happy?" How could you be happy? You bought into it, you've never questioned. That stuff makes me angry.

About My Work

In my plays there's a beginning, middle, and end. There is the story, the conflict, and the resolution of that conflict. Back when I started, a story would just come to me. I was living in a room in Harlem. Like most people, my work is autobiographical. I was really poor. All I could afford at the time was to buy books because I read voraciously. I would read about my dreams. I'd look up what my dreams meant, what they signified. I read guys like Freud and Toni Morrison. So it's from the dream state where I begin to write. I'd try to write the way Francis Bacon painted and the way Jimi Hendrix played. What was I feeling at the time I wrote this? I'd remember my dreams pretty well. I'd ask myself what was I feeling in the dream and then take it from there. Then I'd apply it to where I am now. I can't type, I do all my work long hand. When I first started I was dreaming about being poor, a lot of the colors were very dark colors. Where I used to live were two crack houses and a house of prostitution right across the street. You'd watch chicks in the back alley perform.

So I'd put some words down, some thoughts down, and I'd try to figure out how do I put all of this together? Let's go beyond the dream state; I'd just write what I'm interested in and apply it to that. And that's how it comes about. Names and characters come to me very quickly. The first thing I do is write the monologue, then take it from there. Then I ask myself what is the story within this monologue? I write an outline from the monologue.

How I Work with My Director

I've been a liar and thief and a hypocrite and that's what I tell people. I don't try to make anything, including myself, all nicey. The director is the one who helps me to decide when the piece is ready. The director is the alchemist. I'd bring the director (Peter Askin) what I've written. I'd show him my monologues; I'd say this is the story I want to tell. He helps me to shape it. When I'm reading him the piece, an idea will come to me. He'll say, "Put it in the piece." Peter might say there's too much of this or that. He keeps getting me back to, "What is the story? What is the story?! What is this piece about?" That's kind of it in a nutshell. He'll make me work on what the story is truly about.

We'll look for the event of the piece. Then I'll write toward the event. The process of development is a back and forth, chipping away, as to how the story has to be told. I can be very expositional; we cut a lot of that away.

Other Observations about My Work

I'm not sure when a piece is really ready until I just know. It's something that I feel inside. And that feeling can sometimes occur a month into the show. It's just a gut feeling that it's now happening, really happening.

My process changes all the time. It still starts off initially with my having an idea; something will haunt me. You might say my process is, I don't have a specific process. It really depends on where I am in my life and all that stuff. I only know that when I'm working I don't want anyone near me. I can spend extended periods of time alone; I mean days or weeks.

I don't talk directly to an audience. I'm very aware that they're there. I tell a story and I just hope that they're open enough to hear what I have to say. In a sense I'm saying, here's my vision, my story, my play. I care that you (the audience) hear it. But I'm not going to write something or eliminate something from my story because you may find it offensive or it doesn't apply to your history.

Photo by Greg Gorman

QUENTIN CRISP

Quentin Crisp is a famous wit and celebrated author whose autobiography, *The Naked Civil Servant,* has become a literary classic, as well as an award-winning play and film starring John Hurt. He played Queen Elizabeth in Sally Potter's 1993 film, *Orlando.* Other films include *The Bride, Philadelphia,* and *To Wong Fu, Thanks for Everything, Julie Newmar.* He contributed "The Diary of Quentin Crisp," a column about New York and American culture, to the *New York Native.* He has appeared in television commercials for Levi Straus jeans, Calvin Klein's CK One fragrance, and for Reebok sportswear. Other books include *Resident Alien: The New York Diaries; Quentin Crisp's Book of Quotations: 1000 Observations on Life and Love by, for, and about Gay Men and Women; How to Become a Virgin; How to Have a Lifestyle; Manners from Heaven: A Divine Guide to Good Behavior;* and *Love Made Easy.* His articles have appeared in the *London Times, Newsday, New York Magazine,* the *New York Times,* the *Washington Post,* the *Advocate,* and the *Los Angeles Times.* On television, Mr. Crisp has appeared on David Letterman, Dick Cavett, Jay Leno, Phil Donahue, and Tom Snyder. Mr. Crisp was named one of the "leading thinkers and visionaries" of our time by *Utne Reader.*

- Richard Eder, in the *New York Times,* said, "Mr. Crisp has a valiant and original mind and a lovely way with words. . . . Both in words and in his fussy, faintly self-mocking gestures, he asserts his identity. But what he draws out is universal: gaiety—in the original sense of the word, for once—and themes common to all of us: the need for courage and individuality, and the ground of tragedy on which they are exercised."
- Clive Barnes wrote in the *New York Post:* "[Crisp] is an unexpected and endearing mixture of an off-form Oscar Wilde, an off-beat Dear Abby, and an off-center Will Rogers."

Interview with Quentin Crisp

THE FIRST SHOW

My first show was never actually written down. My agent in England had taken a theater behind a public house (in Islington). In those days there were opening hours, that is to say, from about half past eleven in the morning until half past one or two in the after-noon. And then they shut up for a few hours. Well, my agent took a room behind the pub-lic house in order to put on a show for one of his clients. But he didn't want to waste the lunchtime hours. The stage was small and there was a flimsy curtain. And I agreed to go on for lunchtime. When I asked what I'd do on the stage, he said, "You could talk to people." So there was no script, just impromptu talking. He said you needn't say the same thing each day, just say whatever you want.

At that original show there were about three people in the audience. But every-thing changed when they showed the story of my life on the television (*The Naked Civil Servant*). After that was televised, you couldn't get into the theater, it was so crowded.

Before that televising, I spoke about anything, it was always different. After, I started to make it the same speech. But nothing was ever written down. It was a show with no script, no direction, and no rehearsal.

HAPPINESS

What I spoke about was happiness, because happiness is the only thing that I under-stand. Whatever we say we're talking about, we're really talking about happiness.

Whether we're talking about religion or politics or anything else, we're really talking about happiness. I told people how to be happy, which of course consists of never doing any work. I explained that happiness was never out there, it was always in here. I also spoke about style, about being yourself. I never spoke about myself at all.

DEVELOPING THE SHOW

So I built up, developed this show, so that it had a beginning, middle, and end. The way the show changed was that I altered it in areas that I felt people didn't understand me, what I was talking about. If people didn't laugh at certain jokes, I'd leave them out the next show. I was learning by doing. The entire show was about an hour. The rehearsal, you might say, was the night before's performance. It greatly developed, changed. I always remembered what I did the night before. I'd discuss what it was they could do in their lives to be happy. I don't think they believed me, but they listened.

After I spoke there would be an interval, and the audience would then ask questions. Naturally, that part of the show changed from night to night. By their questions I learned what they understood me to say. That was also a way that I changed the show, by their questions each night.

COMING TO AMERICA

When Mr. Elkins (Hilard Elkins) came to London to see me, I was performing at the Duke of York's theater, which is a real theater (a West End theater). I was performing five nights a week there. The members of the audience who had questions would write them down on cards and I'd answer them in the second half. Mr. Elkins prepared the way for me to do my show in America.

Other than in Australia, where I was asked about my sex life, I was never asked embarrassing questions. But I always, even in Australia, answered them as best I could. I tried to make myself infinitely available to the audience.

Now my show does have a script. It was Mr. Elkins's idea. We recorded one of the shows and the script was typed up from that show. I memorized the script from that recorded show, and that is the show that I now perform, word for word. The second act however, is still questions from the audience. The reason that the show is now better (with a script) is that I don't pause or stop, I continue right through.

GETTING THE AUDIENCE TO LIKE YOU

The way to get an audience to like you is to get them to feel sorry for you. That's what Judy Garland did. When I went to see her perform, that's what impressed me, how she got people to feel sorry for her. I believe that my need is sincere, that is, I do need them to feel sorry for me, just like Miss Garland.

Reby-Stern Photography, St. Louis, MO

MARILYN SOKOL

Marilyn Sokol starred on Broadway as Miss Lynch in *Grease,* in Herb Gardner's *Conversations with My Father,* in *Welcome to the Club* by Cy Coleman and A.E. Hotchner, in O'Neill's *The Great God Brown,* directed by Harold Prince, and in Moliere's *Don Juan,* directed by Stephen Porter with the Phoenix Rep. Her regional theater credits include: *The Sisters Rosensweig, Gypsy,* and *Fiddler on the Roof.* Her films include: Milos Foreman's *Man on the Moon, The Goodbye Girl, Basketball Diaries,* and *Foul Play.* TV credits include: *Law and Order, All My Children,* and *Sesame Street.* Ms. Sokol is an Emmy, Obie, and Bistro Award-winning actress, singer, comedienne, and writer.

- Stephen Holden, in the *New York Times,* wrote, "[Sokol] keeps the audience perpetually off balance as she whizzes between comedy routines and torch songs, trying on different dialects, characters and confessional shticks."
- Nick Popp of *Show Business* said Sokol's one-woman show, *Guilt without Sex . . .* "serves up a . . . theatrical smorgasbord consisting of torchy, tongue-in-cheek song stylings, comedic childhood reminiscences, and a pastiche of incisive and insightful observations about the social, sexual and psychological culture in which we live. The 'world according to Marilyn' is very much her own original."

Interview with Marilyn Sokol

DIFFERENT INCARNATIONS

When I started auditioning after college, I'd go into the auditions, shake the auditors' hands, say hello, and they'd quite often say, "Do you have an act?" I suppose they knew I was a comedienne and assumed that I had an act. At that point, I didn't. But what was bothering me at that time was that I couldn't get to the next rung in my career. I couldn't get the kind of parts that I wanted.

Also, at that time, I was singing around a lot at clubs, and I wanted a record deal. But how do you do it? The solution: You create your own act. I put three songs together and went into Reno Sweeney's nightclub, and got a two-week gig. So I had to quickly put a show together. I couldn't just sing; I had to fill it with stuff, spoken material. So what I did was fill it with characters that I had developed earlier, when I was with the improvisational group, The Ace Trucking Company.

I got together with a friend of mine, Seth Allen, and I would just go over stuff with him. The material was mostly anecdotal, autobiographical. I had a very funny mother. When in doubt, I'd slip into my imitation of her. So all the ideas were mine and then I'd bring in writer friends and actor friends and work with them on the material. Their role was just to bounce the material off them, maybe give me some feedback.

Another friend of mine, Ken Friedman, was a wonderful comic writer; he'd write some punch lines for me. I'd come up with the character and some basic material, and he'd help me to punch it up with punch lines.

To go back a bit, I was always writing, even in college, even when I was a little girl. I was always writing for the page, for the written page. I was prolific in school. It was habitual, part of school work. In college I wrote a lot of creative writing, some autobiographical.

IMPROVISATIONAL WAY OF WORKING

Since I was so improvisational, I found it almost sacrilegious to write down material, to be that scripted. Since I am innately silly, I relied on that rather than some script.

Of course, as the act developed, some nights were funnier than other nights. I would just remember and retain what I did from night to night. There were hardly ever any recordings to rely on. I'd be talking about necking and petting and the first boy I ever did it with, that kind of stuff and much, much more.

I got a gig at the New Ballroom in SoHo; I think it was 1976. It was a twelve-week gig. In preparation for that I got some gorgeous new songs, and I developed some set comic material. That show was more scripted. The words were the glue in that act.

A GOOD EXERCISE

Another exercise that I did, everyday I would just lie down on the couch and let my mind just drift. Whatever came into my mind was fine. No censoring.

GUILT WITHOUT SEX

In the early eighties, I went through a very difficult period in my life. After working a lot of things out, I came out of that period with a stronger sense of self-confidence about my work. I no longer felt the need to have my writer friends come into my rehearsals for their feedback.

Guilt without Sex was a book (unpublished) that I wrote with my friend Ken Friedman. So what I did was I exhumed parts of the book and that was the essence of a new show that I was developing.

This show was entirely scripted. This show also had songs. Some of these songs were originals, some of which I wrote the lyrics for. That show ran on and off for about a year and a half at The Kaufman Theater and the Houseman on Theater Row in New York. I started working with Sue Lawless, a fabulous director. She helped me make it funnier, more entertaining. She also helped me with editing. She helped me with the nipping and tucking of the piece.

THE GREAT VALUE OF ACCIDENTS

There is an incredible value of accidents (artistic accidents). Always use your accidents as an actor. I learned how to repeat them. They can become the funniest parts of your show. An accident is something that you hadn't planned on happening, that happens on stage and ignites something, sometimes a moment, sometimes a lot more. It can be invaluable to an actor. The next show I did was less scripted and once again, more improvisational.

USING THERAPY AS A TOOL

One thing I really feel is that it's very difficult to use autobiographical material such as I did without the help of some kind of introspective discipline. In my case that has been psychotherapy. To loosen unconscious material, deep and understated. The emotional stuff is essentially unusable until some perspective is gained.

Though it's sometimes arduous, this road to self-knowledge is invaluable for an actor or performer, not to mention for life. The stronger the inner connection with your-self, the stronger the connection with the audience. I feel that you need the therapy to loosen it up. Even Uta Hagen says you can't use an emotion, such as something tragic, until you've understood it. You need to work it through. If any actors want to do material from their life, I highly recommend psychotherapy to assist them in their process.

Photo by Chia Messina

EVAN HANDLER

Evan Handler is an actor, author, and screenwriter. He has played leading roles in Ron Howard's film *Ransom* and in *Taps, Sweet Loraine,* and *Dear Mr. Wonderful,* as well as featured roles in Oliver Stone's *Natural Born Killers* and *The Chosen.* Evan has worked on two network television half-hour comedies, *Sibs* and *Whoops.* He is also a veteran of seven Broadway productions, including *Six Degrees of Separation, I Hate Hamlet, Broadway Bound, Brighton Beach Memories,* and the national tour-ing company of *Master Harold . . . and the Boys.* His numerous off-Broadway performances include *Big Al,* at Ensemble Studio Theater (and at The American Jewish Theater); Donald Margulies's *Found a Peanut,* at the Public Theater; and *What's Wrong With This Picture?* at The Manhattan Theater Club. His writing credits include assign-ments for the *New Yorker, Elle Magazine, Mirabella,* and *USA Weekend.* His first book,

Time on Fire: My Comedy of Terrors, an expanded telling of his on-stage memoir, was published to overwhelming positive critical response. The book has been optioned for a film version, for which Evan has written the screenplay. *Time on Fire,* Handler's critically acclaimed one-man show, played to sold-out audiences in New York, Los Angeles, Boston, and Baltimore in venues ranging from a ballroom at Caesar's Palace to the grand stage at Carnegie Hall.

- *Variety* called *Time on Fire* "A powerful punch . . . intelligent and uncompromising, . . . direct, unsentimental and thoroughly engaging. . . . Handler's unswerving recounting always rings true. His conclusion is as rich and contradictory as all that's come before, and one is left hoping that this actor-turned-playwright continues with both endeavors."
- The *L.A. Times* said, ". . . Filled with humor and impressively surrealistic detail, this one-man show is a revelation. Handler is a charming young actor with a wicked sense of humor. The great accomplishment of *Time on Fire* is that he not only survived the ride but also transformed it into a life-affirming act."

Interview with Evan Handler

REASON FOR WRITING

My reason for writing my show was emotionally based. I had been through this jarring experience that was not shared by many people in my age group. I felt like I had a certain amount of isolation that I felt from those involved and attached to the mundanity of their lives. I thought by telling the story of where I had been, this kind of covert war that I had felt that I had fought, that it might actually breach some of the distance between me and the folks that I used to feel close to. At one point I had thought of doing a show where all the doctors were puppets. Anything that would skew the reality and give the otherworldly sense that I had gone through.

THE SIMPLEST WAY

Ultimately, while going through so many ideas of how to tell my story, I always came back to the idea that the simplest one and most direct way would be the most effective. When I actually began working on the show it became my working dictum. I was interested in reducing it to the elements of how I imagined theater must have begun, as people coming together at the end of the day and telling each other where they had been; and how those stories got passed on.

There was something that someone gave me at that time that became a guide. It was a book called *If You Meet the Buddha on the Highway, Shoot Him.* There's a chapter called, I believe, "Disclosing the Self." It was about man's ability to examine where he's been, where he is now, and where he wants to go. It is the telling of the story and the revealing of the self that reveals the self to the individual, as well as forwarding the civilization a fraction of an inch. I became intrigued by that and made it a working guide in writing my piece, and the style in which it would be performed. And I found that it held up to be true. Each night when I went out on the stage to tell my story as directly and simply as possible, there was something that came back to me, and something that the people in the theater left with me.

HOW AND WHY I STARTED

When I was in the hospital, just to combat boredom, I asked my father to get me what was then a really early laptop computer. In the first six months of what proved to be a four-year ordeal, I kept a detailed diary of dreams, of what was going on every day, of the treatment, just about everything. These were just notes. The laptop didn't have a printer. It wasn't 'til years later, when I was working on *Six Degrees of Separation*, that I went to the offices of Lincoln Center and asked them to print my notes out for me. I found some of it to be pretty intriguing, pretty fascinating. I started to write things up, the first five pages or so, and showed it to people at *Six Degrees*. I showed it to Peter Maloney, who was a writer, and to John Guare. And I got encouragement.

TUESDAY NIGHTS AT NINE

At the same time, Naked Angels was doing something called Tuesday Nights at Nine, where people could bring five or ten minutes of stuff they were working on. Eventually I got my nerve up and read the first five pages. It was about ten minutes worth. I got a response that was far better than I ever could have imagined. People howled with laughter and at the same time became appalled at what they were laughing at. That set the tone. I realized that that was the roller coaster ride I wanted to take people on.

LESSONS PREVIOUSLY LEARNED

The literary background that I had prior to this piece was that I had worked extensively as an actor on new plays in developmental situations. I had six summers at the Sundance Institute Playwrights Lab as an actor. I had been around and listened to and heard a lot of the concepts that stuck with me. Things like: It's better to show than to tell. Reveal the story through dramatic action rather than description. Dramatic action comes through conflict. Put the characters into conflict with each other or give them obstacles to overcome, and then show how they do that.

The interesting task for me became, since I'm sitting there and talking by myself, how do I dramatize or show anything dramatically? Everything was description. But I found that there was a way, even within a first person monologue.

WHAT I LEARNED

One thing I discovered was that by inhabiting the characters and having them talking to each other, I could create a present-tense engaging section. I gave the piece a two-act form. Within the two acts, I broke it up into scenes. Each of the scenes revealed specific elements of the story. I gave a lot of thought to structuring the play.

My Agenda, Things I Wanted to Say

I had many agendas in the play. I wanted to show what existed behind the elegant façade of major institutions. I particularly wanted to expose Sloane-Kettering Institute, which was relying on a reputation it had earned three decades earlier. The point was, most people don't know what many of these institutes are like on the inside, unless they've been there. There is no Zagat Guide for hospitals or doctors.

I also wanted to show people that there was more than one way to go through the experience. People are entitled to stand up and fight. I felt a lot of what I went through was a microcosm for the way one decides to go through their life. Most people feel that they're not entitled to all that much, that you must please those in authority and follow the rules.

My play is about one person who had excelled by refusing. The theme of my play is that the world around you tends to demand mediocrity. If you decide to do something to an excellent degree by yourself, there will be a lot of resistance. Today I perform my piece for medical conferences, symposiums, stuff like that. I go to places like Stanford in California, or a conference of four thousand people at the Sheraton in Washington.

Developing the Piece

Going back to the beginnings of the piece. As I mentioned, Naked Angels was doing Tuesday Nights at Nine, where they would assign a topic each week, like religion or money or family. I realized that for any topic they came up with, I could still write about this experience in my life. It was like my weekly soap opera. I went every week with another chapter of five to ten minutes. I didn't work on it every day. But when I did, it could be a six-hour work session. I sat down and wrote. You have to also realize that I had been telling these stories for years prior to the actual sitting down and writing of them. My standing joke was that I'm writing the oral history of me as told to myself. Like any legend or story that's told over and over, I just, in conversation, had honed it and exaggerated it or pinpointed it. Like what you do as an actor, I'd inflate the reality and the drama of the situation without bursting the balloon and going over the line of it being untrue. I would recite it as I read it, as I wrote it. I would recite it over and over, trying to make it fit in my mouth, trying to make it the best story that I could.

Turning It into a Play

So at one point Naked Angels said, "Do you want to do a ninety minute show?" They suggested that I put my pieces together to make one cohesive play. I had a deadline. I had three to six months to do it. I knew the story I wanted to tell, so I started work on the whole play.

I had a clear outline in my head about the shape I wanted it to take. I wrote the whole story down, that was about ninety pages. What I discovered at those Naked Angels nights was that people most wanted to hear what I least wanted to reveal. I discovered that if you're willing to push beyond the bounds of honesty of what most people are willing to give, you've got an edge up on getting their attention and in gaining their respect and interest.

Anybody just telling his personal stuff is not what I'm talking about. You have to find a way to do it that is interesting. I realized that the more personal, honest and I mean scathingly honest, even toward myself, that I made this, people would respond.

When I reached the end of the story, when I was up to today, was when I realized it was ready. When I went to Marcia Jean Kurtz (the director) with the ninety pages, we began to edit it, and we ended up cutting it in half.

REHEARSAL

The way we rehearsed was, I would just start reading the piece. And she would say like, "I don't get this," or "What about this?" or "Why am I hearing this?" or "You're using too many words." So I started to realize that saying something four different times, no matter how cleverly, is not valuable. It's better to pick the most clever of the four and get rid of the rest. This is really about being concise and succinct. I discovered that I was willing to be a ruthless editor of my own stuff. Marcia Jean is one of the best editors I've ever worked with. Marcia Jean was my eyes and ears on the outside. I did rewrites every night at home.

What was interesting about the developing of the piece, the ending kept changing. It seemed that what was going on in my life would suddenly become the ending of the piece. It was like a gift was given. I thought, "Well there you go, I just lived the ending of the piece."

So then I invited everyone I'd known or thought I'd want to know (in the theater world) to the Naked Angels readings (four nights). From that I was offered the Second Stage Theater production.

Between the Naked Angels readings and the Second Stage production, there were some more rewrites. I felt there were a couple of things missing from the text. I incorporated them into the new productions. Then we tried to figure out, how do you put this on a stage, give people their money's worth? I wasn't interested in over-producing this. We started from the place of I'm telling this story to a group of friends in someone's living room. Anywhere that I would stand up to act something out in that environment is where I'll stand up and act something out here. Wherever the story gets worked up enough for you to stand up, then you do. The idea was to keep the story as a story told, as opposed to putting on a show. If I thought something was funny about how someone moved or behaved, then I'd jump up off the couch. I never wanted the feeling, okay, you're coming into a theater, the lights are going down, here's the musical introduction, now I'll take you away to Cancer-land. In fact I wanted to startle people with the simplicity.

EXPERIMENTATION, WAY TO MAKE IT WORK

At the beginning of the run there was experimentation. The producers felt there should be more. They felt people are paying good money to see a show, we should give them something for their money. There was talk about getting another director whose strengths were in lighting and sound design. They felt we should just have "more." But many of their ideas were not what I wanted the piece to be.

I did it in two acts at Naked Angels, and that was very unusual for a monologue show. The joke that I used at the time about the piece was that I called it my "minimalist epic." The whole thing was really about defiance. So I got a kick out of defying what the norms were in the theater. Basically, I had decided that it would work the way I wanted it, despite the conventional wisdom saying it should be more conventional.

MY PERSONAL REACTIONS TO THE PIECE

On a purely personal level, it was terrifying to go out there every night. It felt like I was putting myself much further out on a limb then I ever had before. I felt that if the people weren't liking it, essentially they weren't liking me. On the other hand, it made me feel prouder and more powerful than ever before, because every bit of its success was my success.

In the beginning, I wasn't remembering all my words, so I had little cheat sheets in my pockets. It was a very massive thing. It was written with a literary sense. When I'd go up on my lines, as happened at the beginning, I'd just sit there for a moment, have a moment of terror, and then the next thing would come to me somehow. I'd take a sip of water or something. Mostly, the audience never knew that's what had happened. It became a matter of trusting that the words would come to me.

DEALING WITH THE AUDIENCE

At the beginning, the Second Stage audiences weren't receiving the show very well. Carole Rothman, the producer, felt that it would work better if I told the audience a little about myself first, introducing myself, rather than digging right into the piece. We ended up with me on the edge of the stage, the lights coming up, and me actually introducing myself. A couple of times, I actually started the show with saying, "Hi, I'm Evan." So I did adopt this new beginning of telling a bit about myself. I'd prepare the audience, let them know that this is supposed to be funny, and that it's supposed to be horrible, and that it's okay to experience both.

At least fifty percent of the time at Second Stage Theater, I performed the piece to near total silence. What was odd, was the same piece at Naked Angels was a near raucous laugh riot a lot of the way through. The Second Stage version deprived me of the experience that I wanted to have. But then people would come backstage and tell me how funny the show was. Jerry Zaks (the director) said, "My stomach hurt from holding back the laughs." I asked him, "Why did you?" And he said, "I don't know, it just seemed like what happened out there." It seemed like a great many people that I spoke to at that time were having a similar experience but wouldn't allow themselves to laugh out loud.

There were a lot of walk-outs each night during previews. With an audience of fifty to seventy people, five to ten people would walk out each night. Many of these people were subscription audience people and weren't always aware of what they were coming to see. Many of these people don't want to see a one-person show, let alone a show about cancer. There was a very long preview period. Then the show opened, got this rave review, and sold out immediately. I noticed that once it got the review and people were coming because they wanted to see this particular play, then the response was far better. Every once in a while I would improvise a line or two during the show. If the audience responded well, I'd leave it in. Over the years, there have been quite a few of these add-ons.

MY ADVICE TO WRITERS

For writers everywhere, there is a constant choice to be made regarding those in power and your work. Whether it's a producer or editor or film studio people, you have to decide on what it is you want to say. You must decide how much you're willing to let them influence your choices. I don't mean that there is a constant danger, that these people are out to hurt you. But it is a constant choice to be made. You must decide if what they suggest is helping you to say what you're trying to say. Or is this something that that person wishes this piece was. You must decide, to what extent am I willing to compromise myself? There is a balance to be struck between saying what you have to say and allowing in genuinely good suggestions.

Photo by Tilden Patterson

SHELLY MARS

Shelly Mars has had leads in the *Kids in the Hall Show* and in the HBO special *Drag Kings.* She has had featured and supporting roles in HBO's *Out There Hollywood,* the independent features *Scenes from a Plague Year,* and *Drop Dead Rock.* Her shows *Mars behind Bars* and *Whiplash* have been performed at Dixon Place, the Grove Street Playhouse, and the Kitchen. She's also appeared in shows at Naked Angels theater, New York Theater Workshop (*An Evening of Shelly Mars*), Berkeley Rep, and the Performing Garage. She's appeared on *Montell Williams, The Phil Donahue Show, Real Personal, The Richard Bey Show,* and *The Sally Jesse Raphael Show.*

- Amy Taubin, in the *Village Voice,* called Mars, ". . . an after-hours Lily Tomlin. Mars . . . tells all through precise and subtle body language, tippy toeing between irony and lewdness."
- John Karoly, of *Cab Magazine,* said, "Mars can time a deadpan stare to just the perfect comedic length or let a darker emotion creep subtly across her face during beautifully choreographed pauses in dialogue . . . Mars will thrill, infuriate and arouse anyone who gets to see her work."

Interview with Shelly Mars

STARTING OUT

I started out over fifteen years ago in San Francisco. I was taken to this bisexual bathhouse. There was a striptease contest going on there and my friend dared me to enter it. I did and won the prize. I saw that they did massage in this place. I was like nineteen years old and so I lied to the owner of the place and told him I was older and that I did massage.

So I started working at this bathhouse and started doing shows there. These were crazy, striptease, performance art kind of shows. Actually I had more clothes on than most of the people in the audience. They had like towels on them. I had studied acting and dance and marshal arts, and had incorporated it into my act. I was always a mimic and a character type. People who I found intriguing, I'd mimic and create them as characters.

I was writing to some degree, but mostly just performing and retaining, learning while I was doing. At this time, I didn't sit down like a writer and write. I would usually make up things and bounce it off other people. I incorporated music and dance in my shows too.

DEVELOPING MY FIRST SHOWS

By the time I was twenty-one I had developed my own show which I was doing in a lesbian bar. The show was about Mistress S., a dominatrix. As it developed, it was scripted, but really basic. At this time, I was pretty wild and pretty out there, so my show naturally reflected that. I was extremely rebellious and the show reflected that too. People would say you have to do this or that, and I'd just do whatever it was that I wanted to say at that time. My stuff was very political, very gay. I was exploring gender. I was exploring how repressed gay women were. This was a time when "lipstick lesbians" weren't allowed to exist. I was very opposed to the political correctness of that time. I started doing my male impersonation then. My stuff had a lot of sexual content in it and it really upset lesbians a lot. I always pushed the envelope.

Basically, what I've always tried to say is there are all these variations of the human existence and we're all screwed up. There are all these genders and we need to take on these labels to feel comfortable. I still am talking about that in my present show; it's just a lot more sophisticated now.

DEVELOPING MY PROCESS

I work with a video camera. That came into my process about eight years ago. I work with directors and they'll fish things out of me. I'll be in a persona of a character, and I'll let that persona respond and channel through me into that character. Sometimes things happen in improvisation and then I'll transcribe it. Then we'll make it into something, give it a structure. The artist as editor will decide what works and what sucks.

The director is very important in my process these days. When I was younger, the director was less important. The last few years I've been working with Janice Diner. She's a writer and a film director. She's been important to my writing and helps me with making sense of structure. Her input is very important. She helps things make sense by asking me questions.

ABOUT MY SHOWS

Mistress S. was one of my earliest shows. There were other characters, other actors. Now I do a one-person show with many characters. I guess I do about ten characters, all different ages. For instance, Martin is one of my oldest characters. He is a Wall Street, Merrill Lynch, middle management type. He is a misogynist. My characters evolve with time. What's happening in pop culture affects how they change.

Originally the characters were more broad. They became more specific as they evolved. Owning yourself as an artist really affects your work. Saying, "this is what I do" very much affects the work. I ask myself questions like, "Why are these characters here, and why do I want them to be here?"

As my work progressed, there were lots of *Evening with Shelly Mars* kind of shows. Then came *Invasion from Mars; Whiplash, Tale of a Tomboy;* and *Mars behind Bars,* some of my more recent shows. In *Whiplash, Tale of a Tomboy,* I play my mother, my father, my therapist, and myself. It's the story of how I got to where I'm at. *Mars behind Bars* evolved from that show. That was about your dreams, how you think your life is going to be. It starts out how I grew up in Ohio in a small town, being the only Jewish kid. And how I got the hell out of there when I was seventeen and hitchhiked to South America. Part of the show was about my hitchhiking experiences. How I was raped, then later fell in love with this French girl, Briget. I act all of this out (including the rape).

My work continued on being about my life story and what I thought of it. In the last three years, my work has been much more autobiographical. I now let people know more of who I am, rather than all of the wild personas.

HOW I WORK TODAY

I rehearse a piece a lot. I'll work with the director, do it for him, then call some friends in, do it for them. Everything is scripted now, all my shows. It seems more profession-al. You can go into a theater and give the production people the script and they can see what happens where, technically. It's very helpful to them. I think you should workshop your piece a lot.

The audience is very much a part of the process. Once your homework is done, it really takes life in front of an audience. You can learn so much about what you've created. I'm performing my new work out of town more often these days. Before you get reviewed you want to hone it down and make sure that it's ready. You don't want too much attention on a new piece until it's ready. Yet you need people there. It's a catch-22 kind of thing.

There is a part of me that really knows how to shock people, get their attention that way, push buttons. But there is another part of me that looks really normal, like the girl next door. These personas constantly fight each other. Anger has pushed me for a long time. As I've gotten older, the anger has mellowed, and I find myself more compassionate. But I feel that as an artist you really have to dig in the closets. You've got to let it out. That's what theater's for.

Many years ago I wanted very much to be an actress. I was studying theater, working on scenes, and doing monologues that other people wrote. I hated doing all this stuff (the monologues) that had been done for years. I wanted to do my own thing. I also wanted to do my own thing as a calling card to get recognized. I wanted to be more of a crossover artist like Lily Tomlin and John Leguizamo.

Photo by Lisa Tomasetti (from Penny Arcade Archives)

PENNY ARCADE

Penny Arcade debuted at seventeen with Johnny Varacaro's explosive Playhouse of the Ridiculous. She was a teenage superstar for Andy Warhol's factory, featured in the Morrissey/Warhol film *Women in Revolt.* She has worked with many of the greats of American experimental theater including Jack Smith, Jackie Curtis, Charles Ludlam, H.M. Koutoukas, and Tom O'Horgan, among others.

She began her solo work in 1982. Some of her shows include *While You Were Out* (P.S. 122, New York), *A Quiet Evening with Sid and Nancy* (Chelsea Hotel, New York, En Garde Arts), and *Based on a True Story* (La Mama, New York). Her highly acclaimed show *Bitch! Dyke! Faghag! Whore!* had an international run, playing such places as Melbourne, Australia, Switzerland, Ireland, Scotland, Austria, Germany, and England as well as an extensive run at the Village Gate in New York City. *An Evening with Penny Arcade and Quentin Crisp* was performed at the Vienna Festival as well as in New York.

- Jan Hoffman, in the *Village Voice,* said of *True Stories:* "Ms. Arcade exudes the wry confidence and facility of a veteran downtown performer. . . . Jagged, remarkable, unexpected. And mesmerizing."
- Patrick McDonald, in the *Advertiser,* called *Bitch! Dyke! Faghag! Whore!* "a powerful message wrapped in a challenging package of inspired comedy and gaudy erotica."

Interview with Penny Arcade

Trying to Get a Job

I found myself going out on auditions and the casting directors saying that I was the most original person they'd ever seen in months and months. They said that someday people would be clamoring, "Get me a Penny Arcade. Get me someone like Penny Arcade." After I was told that for about a year and a half, and after getting insignificant roles, I realized I just didn't have time to wait around for people to give me work.

How I Got Started

This was around 1981. The performance art scene at that time was wide open, particularly for women. There was no money in it, but no parameters of what you could and could not do. So, at that time I realized I didn't want to write plays, but I wanted to write stuff that I could perform.

Eventually, I began to write some very large performance pieces, some with as many as thirty people at a time. But I started out just writing for me. I was in a play called *Tinseltown Tirade* at Theater for the New City. The play starred Hibiscus, a famous downtown drag performer. The part that Hibiscus wrote for me was of a Warhol superstar. But he actually didn't know any Warhol superstars. I found that what he wrote was very wooden and unreal. So during rehearsal, for the amusement of other members of the cast, I would improvise on Andrea Whipp, who was a Warhol superstar of the sixties. Eventually he came to me and said, "That's so much better than what I had. Would you mind writing that and we'll give you credit." I went home and looked at a blank piece of paper. I learned that there's a big difference between improvising and writing things. I finally called a friend of mine who was a professional writer and said, "I've been sitting here for four hours and I'm in horrible pain, and the sheet is still blank." And he said, "Oh yeah, you're writing."

I continued to do "Andrea" for a long time. People were always requesting me to do her. I'm a precision mimic for people who I'm interested in mimicking. I can't do anyone on demand, like Pamela Lee Anderson, or someone. I have to really want to mimic them.

Phase Two

I was at a performance art piece at St. Marks in the Bowery. I really hated the piece. So I was in the lobby pacing back and forth, smoking cigarettes, and ranting about how bad it was. Chris Kraus, who was the curator, came up to me and said, "You're fantastic; would you like to do a show here?" I looked at her and said, "What would I do?" And she said, "I hear you write your own material." So I said, "I perform it, I don't write it." She said, "That's fine with me." She gave me a booking.

In my real life I'm always imitating people that I run into. So friends suggested that I do some of those characters on stage. So I did. I actually didn't start writing things down until as late as 1990. The reason I finally did write something down was because I was invited to do one of my monologues at Lincoln Center at a big benefit with Glenn Close, Peter Allen, and all these famous people. I was told that I had ten minutes. Now I never had to time anything, so that's when I decided I had to write this particular monologue down.

The Type of Artist I Am

People often say I'm a political artist. But I'm not a political artist, say, like Judith Malina (The Living Theater). A political artist to me is someone who has a political vision that they want to communicate to the public. So they will write theater in order to use that as a vehicle of communication. I'm a political person so my politics invariably come out in my writing. But that's not my first goal. But ironically at this time of life everything is political. If you flush your toilet it's political. What kind of bottles you choose to buy your drinks in is political.

Today, I feel that the only reason that I perform is to alleviate human suffering and break down self-delusion and isolation.

My Process

Originally, I would tell the same story and the same idea to everyone that I'd come into contact with during the course of a day. That idea came from a sentence I once heard about selling a film treatment. The thought being, if you couldn't pitch your idea in ten minutes, if you couldn't keep someone's interest in that short a time, then you didn't have anything. So, by pitching the idea to ten or twenty people in a day and seeing how they were responding, was how I kind of formed my work. As I said, I started my work by improvising. I have a prodigious memory. So I'd remember most of what I did from night to night.

The Audience

Very early in my career, about 1986–87, I started to feel a tremendous bond with my audience. It was at that time that I was developing my work only in front of an audience. All my work was unrehearsed, unscripted, live, in front of the audience. I felt that from night to night whatever stayed in my memory from the show was worth remembering.

When I started working with other people, however, they insisted that I write things down (for them). That became the difficult part. I'd write for them, but not get around to myself. So they would be fully scripted and my monologues would be fully improvised.

In 1989, I was commissioned by Anne Hamburger (En Garde Arts) to do a piece at the Chelsea Hotel. I chose to do a piece about Sid Vicious and Nancy Sponget. That was the first time I had a piece with other actors. They needed a script to work with. That was a very painful day. I had to write out the entire script for both them and me. It was difficult. I was so used to improvising.

Bitch! Dyke! Faghag! Whore! ran for a year at the Village Gate. I was able to improvise every night, and was able to change it around. At that time, I worked with a dramaturge, Steve Zehenter. He showed me where I was repeating myself. He helped me to develop and shape the show. Ironically, he had no background in theater, whatsoever. He's an architect. It was a sensibility that he had.

I believe the audience is a major player in my work. I often tell them, "I can do nothing for you." I always talk directly to the audience. I always include the audience. I don't feel like I'm more intelligent than my audience. I feel they're pretty much like me. I feel like we're doing it together. They're holding out an end of the tightrope and I'm at the other end. If they believe it, I believe it. If they don't believe it, I don't believe it. Let's face it, people who have an overriding need to perform are not the healthiest people in the world. It's an ego lack. And I like to admit this to the audience. What I get from an audience is a tremendous feeling of acceptance. I'll sometimes tell an audience, "A lot of you might not like me now, but that might change."

Although it might seem self indulgent, I'm really looking for a transformation for myself and my audience every night. I know that I look for a rigorous inquiry when I go to the theater. I expect the same for my audience. You go to the theater to experience what you are unwilling or unable to experience in real life.

SELF-CENSORING

About self-censoring. Sometimes it's intuitive, and not even conscious. You have to always look at "Why am I saying something? What's the real reason?" I always hold myself up to an audience. I'm braver in front of an audience, more honest. Quentin Crisp said a very funny thing. He said, "At a certain point I had to decide how much I was putting on to please myself and how much I was putting on to annoy my mother."

One thing that I learned from Steve (Zehenter) was that by tightening up certain areas, it gave me more room to improvise the rest of the time. If I just group the like-minded thoughts together, then I'd have more room to improvise. I don't rehearse. If I'm in one of my shows with other actors, they rehearse.

MY ADVICE TO OTHER SOLO ARTISTS

My advice to writers of your own material is to use whatever process works for you until it proves otherwise. Even if that process isn't sensible to anyone else. If you start to feel that that process is a cop out or a way of hiding, then it's no longer working well for you.

I remember one way that I used to work was to play specific music over and over. I'd play the same song maybe thirty times in a row. This would put me in to kind of a meditative state that was useful to what I was trying to evoke out of myself.

After a while however, I started to have more respect for the reason why I was doing this, and my process changed. I started to include more people, give up a lot of my unhealthy control. I started to listen to what people said about my work. I'm a very internal person. I think a lot. Then I talk to people about it in my daily life. Then finally I get on stage and talk to the audience. Now I also include feedback from Steve and Eric (my director). That's how I develop my work. My advice to your readers is talk to us about what you're afraid for us to know about you.

www.linda sue scott.com

SHERRY GLASER

Sherry Glaser was a member of the San Diego based feminist improvisational comedy group Hot Flashes, followed by the new age spiritual comedy of the Egomaniacs. Her first solo show was *Coping.* Her next show was *Family Secrets.* Her autobiography, *Family Secrets: One Woman's Affectionate Look at a Relatively Painful Subject,* has been published by Simon & Schuster. Her latest one-woman play, *Oh My Goddess,* premiered at the Michigan Women's and Comedy Festival. Ms. Glaser's one-woman show *Family Secrets* enjoys the position of being the longest running one-woman show in off-Broadway history.

Family Secrets won the Theater World Award for Outstanding Debut. The play was nominated for a Drama Desk Award. She won the Carbonell Award for best actress (South Florida). Ms. Glaser also won the Los Angeles' Outer Critics Circle Award and San Francisco's Solo Mio Award.

- In the *New York Times,* David Richards selected *Family Secrets* as the Critics Choice and said, "Just when you think you know these characters, Ms. Glaser adds another level to their craziness and then another level on top of that. She builds surely and meticulously."
- In *Variety,* Greg Evans wrote of *Family Secrets,* "The well-sculpted monologues, chock full of laugh-out-loud lines and poignant shadings, are delivered with impressive skill."

Interview with Sherry Glaser

STARTING OUT

I was taking an English Lit class that turned out to be an improv class. The professor, Gerry Farber, taught a class called Drama in 3-D. He would do things like turn off all the lights in the class, and say, "You're at a Democratic convention, and you're a hippie at the convention. To one student he'd say, "You're a security guard at the convention." To another, he'd say, "You're just here to flirt," etc. He'd give us all these improvisational assignments. I found my destiny at that time. I learned that I could do accents and that I could do different ages. I learned that I was capable of doing all kinds of neat stuff, and basically that I could really commit to the improv. My goal then, as now, was and is to lose myself in the characters.

Later on, I was doing improvisation in a group called Hot Flashes in the early eighties. We were trying to get away from just doing improvs where you were given an object, a place, or a profession. We wanted to get more into acting and scene work. So we decided to develop characters that could take the suggestions. Most of my work seemed to come from my family. I started reenacting a lot of family stuff. I was very forthcoming with it. During that time I met Greg Howell, who ended up later on being my director and my husband. He inspired me to break off on my own, to go solo.

DEALING WITH LIFE ISSUES IN IMPROV

I wanted to deal with all of the issues in my life. First there was my mother's insanity. The reason that I wanted to deal with it was at that time I felt like I was also going crazy, so that by dealing with it in some expressive way, I could work things out, exorcise the demons, so to speak. Also there were the teenage traumas such as bulimia and drug addiction. There were also wonderful things such as the birth of my child that I wanted to express. The reason that I chose my child's birth was that I had never seen that done on stage before. I had seen feeble attempts at showing childbirth on stage, but never really the whole delivery process.

I also wanted to show falling in love, what that was like. So I created Grandma Rose, who falls in love. I love issues. I find a character and an issue and then I usually find a monologue.

A WAY OF WORKING

I had built up a repertoire of characters. I'd make lists of things that they would talk about, all their expertise. For instance, one character, Sandra's expertise was drugs, boys, parties, eating. Essentially I worked alone at first. I went from improvising the character to making lists of ideas to writing out the script from the improv. Then I'd go out on the stage and just do it.

Sometimes I'd go out there with just an outline and talk. It was limitless since I had so much information on my characters. I'd do these shows in bookstores or in cafés. I had developed a following from my Hot Flashes days. I did about an hour at each show.

My basic style was one character monologue followed by the next one, etc. It was very uneven. Greg would watch and say, "Drop this, move this, try that piece over there." At first the audience was very influential as to how things developed. But then Greg's feedback became more important, and I relied on it. He taught me about silence and drama. I also learned about the ride from laughter to stillness to sorrow. He taught me to trust that, because I'm addicted to an audience's laughter. He was also very influential in the choreography of the piece and the shaping of it. His work was invisible which I think is very important in a solo piece. I think it's important that the direction should not be seen. Greg also co-wrote a lot of the material, especially the jokes. He also gave me the beginning of the evening, that is, how it would start out.

SELF-CENSORING

As for self-censoring, I've really come to terms with it. At the beginning, it was very unnerving. Now I've come to accept it as my friend, and we work together. It's become very helpful. It still hurts though, but it's probably intrinsic to the creative process.

MOVING ON

Harry Weiner, a friend, had seen my show in Monterey. He loved the show but told me that the piece needed a structure, a through-line. I was still just doing characters. He saw the theme, the thread in the piece. He said if you can tie all these characters together, I'll bring you to L.A. I said, "Sure." That opportunity was the impetus, the catalyst that I needed to move from just characters to creating an actual play.

MY REHEARSAL PROCESS

The way that I rehearsed was that I'd run through the whole play, just like you'd rehearse a regular play. I was digging out all the meaning all the time as I rehearsed it. It's funny, but I really had no idea how much I had written until I'd start rehearsing. On the first writing it sounded good, made sense. But then I'd have to find out, "What am I saying here? What am I really saying here?!" My process then as well as today is to unearth the meaning of what I've written.

MAKING DECISIONS

The way the characters were decided became based on how the costumes were going to be. I had to start out with the most difficult costume first. The next costume was right underneath. For other characters, I'd just put on things. Also there was a birth piece which I felt should be the centerpiece of the show. The grand finale had to be the grand-mother monologue, so the pieces just fell into a natural order. Comedy and dramatic choices are also very important in the arrangement of the pieces. Originally there were ten characters when it was at the improv level. Then I developed them down to seven. And finally I pared them down to five.

PERFORMING

To me performing is like having a blind date every night. You're out there and you're naked and anything can happen. Some nights it's like the best sex, and other nights it's like, "How did I get into this?!" It's a roll of the dice all the time.

MY NEXT SHOW

My second show, *Oh My Goddess,* came about from Miguel, a character that didn't make it, was cut from the first show. He wanted to do a show. I created "Ma," the ultimate Jewish mother, for this new piece. It feels like the entire show, especially Ma, was channeled to me. I believe a lot of actors creating their own material will sometimes feel that material is channeled. It's one of the wonderful parts of this type of work. What happens in the new show, Miguel channels the goddess. He tells the story of how he got to be the channeler. It's been a lot easier this show than the first. At the ending of the show I answer questions as Ma. It allows me to do my improv again. It's so easy; I can say anything. Both Miguel and Ma are forty-five minutes each. In this show I try to work out the death of my father. I've been working on this show for about two years. This show found me, whereas the first show I had to look for.

At first I was very resistant to doing another show, but then I decided, what the hell. Let me say, it takes a lot out of you to do one of these. There is the fear to deal with, and all the preparation. It takes its toll on your body too. Now, the new show, there are only two characters and that makes me so happy; it's a lot easier. It's not nearly as demanding.

SOME ADVICE FOR ACTORS

The only advice that I have for actors who want to write their own material is always be aware of details, little details. The more specific you are, the more rich the material will be. Also, if you can express the truth of what you're feeling in the situation, in the moment, the material will work a lot better. I personally like to go on an emotional trip. Use the outstanding, unresolved parts of your life as fodder for the material that you want to create. It's helpful if you have some distance from upsetting events you want to write about. They shouldn't be too new. But the most important thing, you have to be honest at all times up there. The audience will know if you're telegraphing the performance in.

KATE CLINTON

Copyright 1999 Carol Rosegg

In 1993, Kate Clinton's first one-woman show, *Out is In,* debuted in Los Angeles to sold-out crowds. The show then moved to New York for a three month run off-Broadway. In 1995, her next one-woman show, *Impure Thoughts,* debuted in Los Angeles. Her next show, *All Het Up,* toured the country in 1996. Ms. Clinton joined *The Rosie O'Donnell Show* as a television writer seeing them through their initial launch and roll-out period. She has appeared on Comedy Central, *Good Morning America, Nightline, CNN, C-Span, Entertainment Tonight, Arsenio Hall,* TV Food Network, FX, and PBS. She also hosted *In the Life* and collaborated on *The World According to Us,* which aired as three specials on the Lifetime network. Ms. Clinton has five comedy albums to her credit. Her book, *Don't Get Me Started,* was published by Ballantine, and is presently in its fourth printing. She writes a monthly column for the *Progressive,* and has written pieces for the *New York Times,* the *Advocate,* and *George Magazine.*

- Ben Brantley, in the *New York Times,* said, ". . . while Ms. Clinton may exude a raffish professional polish that fits comfortably within a conventional talk show format, she never forsakes a certain sunny subversiveness. Metaphorically, she always carries a knife: only a dinner knife, perhaps, but its edge is never blunt."
- Sharon Schatz, of the *Los Angeles Times,* said, "[Clinton's] quick wit and hilarious antics, combined with an endearing maternal style, make even the potential homophobes in the audience want to take her to lunch by show's end."

Interview with Kate Clinton

STARTING OUT

My material is topical and occasional. What I mean by occasional is that it's for different occasions. I write a lot of political stuff. Generally, the political material is at the beginning of each routine. It usually changes with almost every show.

I started out in 1981. I was doing these readings with this women's writing group I was in. I would intentionally go for laughs to help with the maudlin aspect of some of the heavy stuff a lot of these ladies were writing. At that same time, I had been talking about trying to do stand-up comedy. I think I told my best friend too many times that I wanted to try stand-up, because she booked me into a club. It was a club in Syracuse. She called me and said, "You're on in a month." That's how I started. That first piece was just to amuse, to see if I could get laughs. I like to say I was translating Adrienne Rich into one-liners. In case you don't know who she is, she's a wonderful but definitely very serious feminist writer. Rich had written a huge piece about compulsory heterosexuality. I condensed it into one line about the penis with a mind of its own.

How I Work

Because I had been a high school English teacher, I had developed a way of working. I wrote and clipped and cut material for my shows, just as I had in school. Also, I would try out the material with people at dinner. And I'd read things to my partner. I discovered that although I'd written a two-page piece of material, after performing it once, I could cut it down to one or two lines, based on a person or audience's reaction. I would watch to see how people reacted to my material, and that was a strong determining factor of how it would change. So to be precise, I'd write it down first, and then I'd take it out into the field and try it out. The try-out phase for new material would usually be about a year.

The first piece I performed publicly was thirty-three minutes long. I called one hundred and eighty of my closest friends and trusted codependents to come see it. It went fine. They were all the people I had amused at parties, except now they had to pay.

The Second Show and What I Learned

Actually, the second show that I did was more revealing to me. It was in Boston at an alternative theater space. These were people that I didn't know. What was interesting was that two weeks before, I had gotten uproarious laughs at a particular line, but that night there was dead silence. From teaching I knew not to panic. I just kept going on. Again, there was another line that two weeks before I had gotten a lot of laughs on. But that night, again, nothing, silence. I must have had a stricken look on my face because I heard a voice from the audience say, "You're on your own darling." The lesson of course is, you are on your own, and you just must keep going.

How My Material Has Developed

Within six months of that first show my shows were running ninety minutes. My material is arranged like a newspaper. I always start out with a kind of welcome in the beginning. I next locate where we are, a comment on the hall itself. I like to spy on the crowd as they're coming in. I'll talk about them. It's a way of locating us. After that, I discuss the news of the day, front page. There's sports, there's media, culture comments, editorials, science news, etc.

Because I wasn't performing in comedy clubs, I wasn't gearing my material with jokes and punch lines. I worked more with anecdotes, observations, that kind of thing. I always end my show with some sort of farewell material, which has varied during the years, but generally is a more serious material. In the beginning, I worked a lot in church basements. Later on, I moved upstairs in the church. I must say the Unitarians really moved my career along. I've also worked in coffeehouses. Now I do concert halls. The way that I used to rehearse was, I worked in front of my blue couch. I pictured imaginary people sitting there. My best friend was there; I'd imagine Lily Tomlin, Dorothy Parker, all kinds of folks. I'd rehearse my material to them, imagine their reactions.

THESE DAYS

These days in my show, I'm talking a lot about mergers, how everything's merging. Banks are merging, oil companies are merging, like that. I mention how gay and straight people seem to be merging. And also I mention that I've noticed how the world is going very fast these days. Maybe because of everyone drinking too much coffee. Money, media, and sports interest me and I also include those subjects in my shows. I often feel like I'm an anthropologist.

My new show feels particularly like that. When I think of my process of working on material, I think of the way I developed my work as a teacher. When I first started teaching, I would write out almost everything, word for word, what I was going to say in class. But by the time I stopped teaching, years later, I was lucky if I wrote just one or two words to remind me what I'd be teaching the next day. I'd stopped writing out everything and would just wing it. At the beginning of my monologue work, I wrote out every sentence. That eventually evolved to just a simple set list of what I was going to talk about. There was a real script for me, which I'd automatically memorize. If there's a lot of new material, I'll put a set list down, which I take with me on the stage. I no longer rehearse with imaginary people on a blue couch. They've sort of become internalized now. As I said, I try things out on people all the time. I depend totally on the audience for feedback. I don't have a director; I never have.

WHAT PERFORMING IS LIKE FOR ME

For me, performing my material is a legal high. I did a show at Town Hall (New York) once that was spectacular. I remember getting off that stage and going, "Yes!" I still see people on the street who say to me, "I was at the Town Hall show." And I'll say to them, "Well then, you saw the show." They know exactly what I mean. I felt like I had actually levitated during that show, that's how high it made me feel. It's like you do all the hard work, you prepare and then sometimes, like on that night, it felt like it was just coming right through me. My timing was wonderful, everything seemed to work perfectly.

I don't do characters, say, like Lily Tomlin. But every so often when I'm on stage and I hear myself doing voices, I know something special is happening out there. The material is taking me somewhere. I don't write character monologue material per se. But in the stories that I tell, I will sometimes deliver a line as the character. I do sound effects though. I find myself doing them to enhance a story. I've always loved doing sound effects, even as a kid.

WHAT I LEARNED FROM BEING A TEACHER

Talking about audiences, I'd like to go back to how teaching affected my work. When I was a teacher, on some days I'd teach like five classes. Three of those classes might be the same thing. If something went really well in the first class, I'd try to do it in the second and it would just fall into place, because it had now become spontaneous. And what I learned there was you can't have any expectations, you have to go with what's presented to you. You present and then you get a reaction, and that's what you can't predict. In performing, I find that also true. I find that if I'm prepared enough, I can improvise from what I've prepared.

MY PRESENT SHOW

On the show I'm now working, I'm at a point where I'm just taking notes. This show feels like it will be transitional. I'm making myself write more personal things. I'm working with these blue index cards that are all over my desk. They are notes of interesting phrases or historical things that have occurred. Right now I'm in a process of discovery and serendipity. I make myself work on the material for four or five hours every day. I'll sit around and think about what I want to say, then I'll write out some of the thoughts, and then I'll go to my computer and type it up and then print it out and take a look at what I've got. There will be things on the page that kind of vibrate, visually. And when that happens I know it's something I want to pursue. So I'll underline those things. I'm interested in entertaining people, but I'm also interested in the political scene. I'm interested in changing people's minds about things. I hope that when I'm much older that I'll still be talking about things that will change the system a bit.

17

INTERVIEWS
WITH DIRECTORS OF
ONE-PERSON SHOWS

These were the general questions that I asked of all the directors that I interviewed. Some additional questions were asked depending on the director's individual responses.

- What drew you to directing the first one-person show you worked on?
- As you started rehearsing, what differences did you notice between working on solo shows and on a regular play? Were there any things that came up that you hadn't anticipated?
- How would you describe the relationship between you and the actors in the solo shows you've worked on? How was it different than working on a regular play?
- Can you describe the way you like to rehearse, develop these plays?
- How did you shape the material with the actors you worked with? Did that change much from performer to performer?
- How do you decide when the material is ready?
- What similarities and differences have you noticed between the solo shows you've worked on?
- From a director's point of view, what advice do you have for actors who are thinking about writing their own solo shows? Any other comments that you'd like to make regarding solo shows?

Photo by Joan Marcus

PETER ASKIN

Peter Askin directed and developed the award winning off-Broadway productions of John Leguizamo's *Mambo Mouth* and *Spic-O-Rama,* and Dael Orlandersmith's *Beauty's Daughter.* Other off-Broadway directing credits include *Reality Ranch, Beauty Marks, Reno,* and the New York and Pasadena Playhouse productions of *Down an Alley Filled with Cats.* He directed *The Gimmick* at the McCarter and the Sundance Film Festival, and the highly acclaimed rock musical *Hedwig and the Angry Inch.* For television, he directed the HBO production of *Spic-O-Rama,* and was the supervising produc-

er for John Leguizamo's Fox comedy series *House of Buggin'.* He also collaborated with Mr. Leguizamo on the Comedy Channel's *Talent Pool.* Peter co-wrote *Smithereens,* the film that was Susan Seidelman's directorial debut. He is directing Sigourney Weaver, John Turturro, and Woody Allen in *Company Man,* a film he co-wrote with *Bullet's over Broadway* and *Emma* writer, Doug McGrath. *Mambo Mouth* won an Obie and Outer Critics Award, *Spic-O-Rama* won the Drama Desk Award and several Cable Ace Awards, including Direction of a Comedy Special (TV). *Beauty's Daughter* won the Obie and *Talent Pool* won a Cable Ace Award. He wrote "What Are You, Stupid?" for HBO's *Peace: Live It or Rest in It.*

- Clive Barnes, in the *New York Post,* said, "*Spic-O-Rama* has been expertly directed by Peter Askin, who is also credited with 'developing' the show, so presumably had some creative hand in the deal. Don't miss it!"
- Ben Brantley, in the *New York Times,* said, "Under Peter Askin's slick direction, Mr. McGrath emerges as an agile, confident performer, capable of shifting roles with ease."
- Peter Marks, also in the *New York Times,* said, "[In] *Hedwig and the Angry Inch,* Michael Cerveris is superbly directed by Peter Askin."

Interview with Peter Askin

STARTING OUT—HOW TO TALK TO ACTORS

My first one-person show was a play called *Reno* with Paul Zimmerman. I directed it at The West Bank Café and later on at the Acme Bar and Grill. I was very attracted to the material. It had a dark bite to it, dark, dark humor. One thing I learned working on that show was how to talk to actors. I had been a directing student with Wynn Handman, and was now learning to apply some of my new skills.

Previous to this, I had been a writer. So what I brought to directing was a writer's eye in terms of structure. The thing I still bring and concentrate on initially is dramaturgy. I feel that it is such a luxury to work one-on-one with the writer-actor. You can focus on minutiae both in performance and on the page. The goal, at least for me, is to get it as close to what I think it can be on the page. Then, when you start rehearsal you have a stronger platform.

What Actor-Writers Must Learn

Dramaturgically, I don't think there is that much difference between a one-person play and a multi-character play. Both still need structure. One of the pitfalls authors of one-person shows have is that their stuff is not always in dramatic form; it's too narrative and expositional. To make things dramatic, you have to place things in the present tense. You have to look for conflict.

Differences between a Regular Play and the Solo Play

Since there is just the two of you in development of a one-person show, the actor has to trust you. In a play, the actors in rehearsal feed off each other. A one-person show is a much lonelier proposition, particularly for the actor. He's in a much more vulnerable position. Actors in a regular play rely on each other to create; in the one-person show the actor only has the audience as his partner. If the actor in a multi-character play is off or flat, in a certain beat or moment (especially in the beginning), another actor can rescue him.

It was always interesting to watch John Leguizamo, who, like many actors, relates to laughter like food. The shows would vary from performance to performance, depending on the audience's response, in itself always a variable. *Spic-O-Rama* could be shortened by as much as two or three minutes if the audience wasn't responding that night. John would go faster because he was not getting the laughter he wanted. His performance would get a shade angrier, which would also speed things up.

Working on *Mambo Mouth*

I first saw the show at Intar on Forty-second Street. It had elaborate costumes and changes could take five minutes between monologues. It was mainly a question dramaturgically of shaping, condensing, combining, and eliminating redundancy. I worked with him on shaping the monologues so they'd have an arc. We worked to illuminate the monologues, to find what a monologue was really about. The best example of this was the *Crossover King*. It was the last monologue of the evening, a Japanese businessman. Originally, I believe the fun for John was playing a Japanese character. What seemed obvious to me though, after we read it through two or three times, was that this was about a Hispanic, who put on the guise of a Japanese businessman. His dilemma was that the Japanese corporate shell could not contain the emotions of the real person, the Hispanic, from bursting through in opportune moments. Once we realized that, then it was easy because that's what it was about.

To make the transitions interesting in *Mambo Mouth,* I hit on the silhouette idea. The characters would finish a monologue behind a scrim. And as John changed costumes, he'd keep talking as the end of one character fed into the beginning of the next monologue behind the scrim. The order of the characters, to some extent, depended on those transitions.

I wanted *Mambo Mouth* to have some kind of common thread, if possible. So we imposed a network of relationships. It was mainly for us, but the cross references helped unify the evening's landscape.

WORKING ON *SPIC-O-RAMA*

I mainly want to tell a story in a one-person show, rather than just have an actor showing his craft. With *Spic-O-Rama* we created a family. John was still going to do different characters, but now there was an event, the marriage of one of the brothers. The precocious kid who opened the show introduced us to all of his family members. He provided the through-line. Each monologue reflected on the event.

The way the stage was used was determined by the story or the play. John, like Eric Bogosian, could have done *Spic-O-Rama* in street clothes. But he enjoyed using costumes. The most important thing for me was speed between scenes. *Spic-O-Rama* had a much more ambitious set, kind of a warped reality, representing elements from the Gigante life.

WORKING ON *POLITICAL ANIMAL*

Another one-person show I directed was Doug McGrath's *Political Animal.* That show used video. Once again, the story dictated the set. It was a political satire involving a television interview with a particularly greasy Republican presidential candidate. So we used the idea of the television interview. We taped Doug doing the candidate being interviewed. That was the thread throughout the play because we kept coming back to that interview. There were four TV monitors on the stage. As Doug began another character, we'd go to the television video of that character. We'd begin a scene on those monitors. As soon as he was in costume change we'd go from the monitors to him live. *Political Animal* was one story with twelve characters.

WORKING ON *HEDWIG AND THE ANGRY INCH*

I had never seen *Hedwig and the Angry Inch* before, although they had done several performances before I got involved. I also had never worked on a musical before. I was struck by the intelligence of the writing, a combination of broad stand-up and very smart storytelling and songwriting. Still the first thing again was dramaturgy. It was kind of all over the place, hard for the audience to follow. I worked on clarifying it. We broke it down into two acts. Once we did that it was easy to build toward the end of each act.

Working with Dael Orlandersmith

Working with Dael Orlandersmith was different because she's primarily a poet. We worked together very closely on developing her pieces. She writes very close to the bone, based on her own experience. The three pieces we worked on were *Beauty's Daughter, Monster,* and *The Gimmick.* Her writing can be repetitive; she comes back to the same themes. What freed Dael up was when I introduced her poetry into *Beauty's Daughter,* then found this poetic narrative voice, a form she is writing in now which is unique to her. It has all her strengths; she writes much more freely.

How the Rehearsal Processes Varied

The rehearsal process with John Leguizamo was fascinating for me. I learned so much about acting from him. It was simply a question of having an idea, communicating it to him, and then watching him make it his own. You just watch it grow. He has the tools, these extraordinary gifts as an actor. Not only is he a comic, he's also a stunning dramatic actor.

Doug is a highly skilled writer and one of the funniest people alive. I did a lot less dramaturgical work with Doug, and when I'd give him an idea, he'd grasp it very quickly. He grew a great deal as an actor during rehearsal.

Dael is a powerhouse, a force of nature. We trust each other and are friends. But I'm much tougher on Dael than anyone else. What was a bit more difficult with her was that she was always writing and memorizing during rehearsal. It was a slower process. She's a very strong actor, and, once she has an idea, she has the capacity to build on it.

John Cameron Mitchell is an extremely bright actor and writer. *Hedwig* was an ambitious play, drawing inspiration from elements as unlikely as Plato's *Symposium.* John and Stephen Trask had lived inside of it too long and simply needed a fresh perspective they could trust.

Knowing When It's Ready

The way you know when the one-person show is ready is similar to knowing when a regular play is ready. Does it build? Are there flat moments? Is there redundancy? Is it clear?

When those questions are answered, you get a sense of where the piece is. It's a living thing like any play. It's going to be a lot different in the third week than the first. If the actor's still trying to solve writing problems in previews, then he'll never have a chance to be able to expand it, play, and grow.

MY ADVICE TO ACTOR-WRITERS

For actors who want to write their own shows, the only advice I have is, think hard and long about the story you want to tell. Spend a lot of time on the written part of it. I know that a lot of actors like to work out of improvs. If that's the case, you still have to develop your story; it's just a different methodology. You need someone with you whose eye you trust. It doesn't have to be a director, just someone who can help clarify the story, the through-line, or the structure. Break the piece into three acts and give each a structure. If you want to write characters, find the story you want to tell with these characters. Think of each character as a dramatic (comedic) story. Tell the story in the present tense. Find conflict within the monologue.

Photo by Paula Cort

JO BONNEY

Jo Bonney most recently directed the highly acclaimed premiere of Diana Son's *Stop Kiss* at the Public Theater in New York. She also directed Danny Hoch's *Jails, Hospitals and Hip-Hop* at P.S. 122, Philip Ridley's *The Fastest Clock in the Universe*, and the premiere of Seth Zvi Rosenfield's *The Flatted Fifth* at The New Group. She directed Eric Bogosian's *Suburbia* at the Studio Theater in Washington, D.C., Karen William's *How I Got to Cleveland* with Robert Olen Butler's *Fairly Tale* at P.S. 122, Patrick Breen's *At Midnight and Morning Rain*, and Warren Leight's *Stray Cats*, both at Naked Angels. She directed Eric Bogosian's *Funhouse; Sex, Drugs and Rock and Roll; Pounding Nails in the Floor with My Forehead;* and his current work in progress. At The Public Theater, she directed Danny Hoch's *Some People*. Ms. Bonney is Associate Artistic Director of The New Group in New York. Jo Bonney is the recipient of the 1998 Obie for Sustained Excellence of Directing.

- Of Ms. Bonney's direction of Eric Bogosian's *Wake Up and Smell the Coffee*, Robert Hurwitt, in the *San Francisco Examiner*, said: "Bogosian's solos (as opposed to plays like *Talk Radio*) seem both carelessly thrown together and crafted with exquisite care by the writer-performer and his director, wife, and longtime collaborator Jo Bonney."
- Michael Feingold, in the *Village Voice*, said, of Bonney's direction of Danny Hoch's *Some People:* "It's in these complex pieces that Jo Bonney's discreet direction comes subtly into play."

Interview with Jo Bonney

STARTING OUT IN THIS TYPE OF WORK

I didn't come out of theater. I came out of visual arts, arts and design. So I didn't make a decision to direct my first solo show. I had started working with Eric Bogosian. I had hired him to do a voice-over for a short film I was making. It was around 1980. He had just started creating his solo shows. It was a particular time when a lot of people were making solo shows. So I started directing his work simply because we were working on a lot of projects together at that time. I directed all of his shows, from *Funhouse* to *Sex, Drugs and Rock and Roll* to *Driving Nails in My Forehead.*

USING MY BACKGROUND TO WORK ON SOLO SHOWS

Even though I started out in visual arts, I had always worked in graphics so I had done some work in TV and video. I had directed shorts, many using actors. So working on a one-person show was very manageable for me. Also, I spend a lot of time on these shows as an editor-dramaturge. I don't come in at the end when the piece is already written. I come in at ground-zero, at the beginning, when the piece is just starting to be written. That's how I've always worked with Eric and Danny (Hoch). For me that's always half the pleasure. For me, directing, that is, blocking a piece, is only about 25 percent of the work. The rest of the work is working with the dialogue. I know a lot of other directors of one-person shows who come in when the piece is already written. They help by editing and staging it. It really just depends on who you're working with, the relationship you have established, the trust, the sensibilities, etc.

THE DIFFERENCE BETWEEN SOLO SHOWS AND ENSEMBLE PIECES

I would say the main differences between working on a solo show and a regular play have to do with whether the piece is scripted (as in most plays). With a scripted play, you just apply your vision to the piece. As I mentioned, with a solo piece, I come into the collaboration very early on, at the beginning. My work is similar when working on a new play and working on solo material. In both cases, I help develop the material. I'm part of the creation of the show.

I worked on a play a couple of years ago (for The New Group) that was already completely scripted. It was a very different process than working with a play's development. I personally love the interaction, the collaboration, with the writer in a play's growth.

WORKING WITH THE WRITER-PERFORMER

When you're working with an actor in a solo piece, they're also the writer, the originator of the material. There's a lot of conversation as to perhaps the tone is off, or if the structure is working, etc. You have to split the writer from the performer. The writer is in love with the words, and the performer is in love with the audience. My job, I've always felt, is tempering both inclinations so that they can work together. With the writer, you just have to be ruthless and just eliminate where the writing isn't working. If they trust you, they'll go with your choices and what you're seeing. They know that my job is just to make them look better. My work with the writer-performer is to make them look fabulous on that stage, so that I just disappear into the woodwork.

In ensemble work, the director's hand is more in the forefront. Working with solo performers is very intense, very mind-to-mind. If you like that other mind, it's really fun; you're both in the sandpit together. I'm very selective about who I work with on solo work because it's a very demanding commitment. It's a shared sensibility. These pieces can take nine months to complete. There's the editing, the workshops, then out on the road, then you bring them in for a run, a lot of time and energy.

I should mention that I'm very writer-oriented. I want the pieces to read as really strong literature on the page as well as in the performance. That's not the case with all solo work. A lot of solo work is very body-oriented or dance or cabaret or performance art. I mainly work with people who come out of a theater tradition.

The Technical Aspects of the Solo Show

One of the main areas that I work with technically, in solo work, is lighting. The work that I do uses minimal set and props. This isn't always the case with other artists' solo shows. There is a huge range of solo work. Some are very prop, costume, and set intensive. Some use video screens, multimedia, etc.

What I like about the solo work that I do with Eric and Danny is the quick change from character to character, and the quick change in body language and voice; you're suddenly in another place and time with another character. The less clutter there is around, the more amazing the transformation.

My Feelings about Solo Work

A solo piece is a very delicate piece. It's really about the energy and personality of the performer. And more than anything it's about the energy between the performer and the audience. So actually I spend a lot of my time once we have gone through the sitting in a room, you know, scanning the writing and ideas, out in the back of the audience. I watch the audience as much as I watch the performer. I try to gauge where it's connecting and where it's reading and where it's going off, and what the audience's reaction is.

Working with Eric Bogosian and Danny Hoch

Danny, Eric, and I have a similar work situation. Both of them came out of theater as actors, not as writers. Initially, when they were both doing their work, they'd get up on stage, unscripted. Much of the work was in their heads, and they'd improvise. When I started to work with Eric, and then later with Danny, I told them, "I can't direct you if I don't have something on paper, it's way too ephemeral." So at a certain point, they both started scripting their pieces, transcribing them, writing down work that had simply existed in their heads before.

Before we would actually go to a rehearsal room, we'd just meet and discuss what's on the page. In some cases it was a fully birthed character. Then I'd just say, "Let's see him on his feet." Then I'd watch and decide whether I felt it needed cutting or something, or whether it didn't need any playing with. For another character, in a whole page of writing, I might find that there may be just one fabulous line of writing. So you start from that and say, "This line makes sense and the rest should just go. The rest is just punching in the dark." Then we'd play around with that, improv on that, and then they'd go away, do some more writing.

In the past, Eric has used a tape recorder in order to feel more spontaneous. He felt he might not get that spontaneity if he was sitting, just writing. Then I'd listen to the recording and see if there was a line or direction that seemed interesting. Eric hasn't worked, however, with a tape recorder in a number of years, but at one point he felt it was useful.

One thing I've noticed about Eric and Danny over the years is that they've become better and better writers. So the flow from the brain to the hand has become almost as organic as if they were really saying the line. Another thing, Eric and Danny will both jot things down as it comes to them, stuff that they might want to look at later. It's a very free-fall kind of process. They'll improv, they'll write, they'll show me stuff, put it up, go back, I'll do some editing, they'll write some more, they'll workshop it, then there's a point where they'll put it up in front of people. It's not a clean-cut, black-and-white kind of process. It's very circular.

Deciding When It's Ready, Developing the Piece in Front of an Audience

We never sit and decide, "this piece is ready now." What we do is, we get to the point where we arbitrarily decide a time to set it up and put it in front of an audience. We'll put it up at P.S. 122, or at the Knitting Factory or at any space. The criteria is you decide that you have an hour's worth of work that you're ready to have seen. We make it clear to our audience at that time that this is a work in progress. The first workshops are just the embryos. You might see some characters, some ideas. But as the workshops continue in the course of a few months, you'll see them grow. Some characters might drop out completely, others may suddenly appear.

Sometimes I'll see something in one piece, then something in another that isn't quite there. But if you put the two pieces together you can create a more complex character. The way you know when it's set is that the character is satisfying to you, the show has the shape and the arc that you want it to have, the piece has the right rhythms from the beginning to the end. You just have to trust your instincts.

The beginning and end characters are often quite tricky to decide on because you're trying to find what dynamic you start and finish on. You also want to make sure that whatever you lead with really sets your audience's mind in a particular place. In Danny's most recent show, *Jails, Hospitals and Hip-Hop,* there's a rap piece that used to be at the end, but then we finally decided that it should be at the beginning. We realized that its message was too heavy, that it was more interesting at the top of the show.

THINGS TO KEEP IN MIND WHEN CREATING A SOLO SHOW

By the end of the show, where do we want to take the audience? How do we get there? Like a dance or music piece, there is a rhythm to a show. It's how you hear it, see it. You're juggling a lot of things when deciding which piece goes when. Pacing also is a factor to consider. There are different dialects and languages in these shows that the ear has to catch up to. You also have to give the audience's ears a chance to relax because it's often such a diatribe coming at them, a wall of words. There's also comedic versus dramatic pieces to consider. There are so many factors to constantly keep considering in the formation of the whole evening.

SOME OTHER ADVICE

Solo shows are a personality-driven form. It's difficult to mention rules because it's so individual. If your interests or personality go toward a more mythical-fantastical storytelling, then that's the kind of show you should make. If you have an ear for urban dialect, and you get off on those rhythms, then you should go toward creating characters. It should always have an energy that's about theater. The worst kind of shows are where a person is just telling the story of their life, where they think people will be interested in their paranoias or dilemmas.

ADVICE TO DIRECTORS OF SOLO SHOWS

As far as directors doing these shows, you must really love that intense one-on-one collaboration with another artist. You must be the kind of director who can sit on your ego in the end, because it really does, in the final moment, become the phenomenon of the solo performer.

ADVICE TO ACTORS

My advice to actors is, if you're working on your own material, you should find a director that you really trust to work with you at some point. It's very difficult to do this kind of work all alone. Having an objective eye on your work can be immensely helpful.

CHRISTOPHER ASHLEY

Christopher Ashley's solo shows include Anna Deavere Smith's *Fires in the Mirror* at the New York Shakespeare Festival, Claudia Shear's *Blown Sideways through Life* at New York Theater Workshop and the Minetta Lane Theater, and Dario Fo's *Tale of the Tiger* at New York Theater Workshop and the Minetta Lane Theater. Other New York credits include *The Most Fabulous Story Ever Told* at the New York Theater Workshop and the Minetta Lane Theater, *Jeffrey* at the WPA and Minetta Lane Theater, *Communicating Doors* at the Variety Arts Theater, *L'il Abner* for Encores at City Center, *Das Barbecu* at the Minetta Lane Theater, *Bunny, Bunny* at the Lucille Lortel, *As Thousands Cheer* for the Drama Deptartment, *The Naked Truth,* and *The Night Hank Williams Died,* as well as numerous plays at the WPA. Regionally, he has directed at American Repertory Theater, Center Stage in Baltimore, Cincinnati Playhouse in the Park, George Street Theater, Goodspeed Opera House, Intiman Theater, Long Wharf, Williamstown Theater Festival, Los Angeles Theater Center, New York Stage and Film, Philadelphia Theater Company, The Royal George in Chicago, Shakespeare and Company, and Westside Arts in Los Angeles. His film work includes *Blown Sideways through Life* for American Playhouse (PBS) and *Jeffrey* (for Orion Classics). Mr. Ashley won the Lucille Lortel Award for Outstanding Direction of *Fires in the Mirror* and *Jeffrey.* For *Jeffrey,* he won an Obie award, two Dramalogues and a San Francisco Bay Area Critics Award.

- Clive Barnes, in the *New York Post,* said of *Blown Sideways through Life,* "Ms. Shear has what used to be called the gift of gab, and, aided, abetted, developed, and directed by the extraordinarily talented Christopher Ashley . . . "
- Frank Rich, in the *New York Times,* said, "*Blown Sideways* may not be a play, exactly, but it merits the elegant full-dress production that it has received from the director Christopher Ashley."

Interview with Christopher Ashley

The two most well-known one-person shows that I've done are *Blown Sideways through Life,* written by and starring Claudia Shear, and *Fires in the Mirror,* written by and starring Anna Deavere Smith. I directed both of these shows at almost the same time, but I believe *Fires in the Mirror* came first.

Working with Anna Deavere Smith on *Fires in the Mirror*

I believe *Fires in the Mirror* was the first piece in Anna Deavere Smith's documentary-type series. I didn't know Anna before I was asked to do that piece. For me, the hook there was the material; it was so interesting, so fresh, so innovative. Also, her way of working was so interesting. This whole thing happened during Joanne Alkalitis's tenure at the Public Theater. I had assisted Joanne on one of those TCG NEA grants a couple of months before. Anna had done a workshop of *Fires in the Mirror* and was hunting around for a director. I didn't see the original workshop that Anna had done at the Public.

Originally there was, believe it or not, about nine hours of material for *Fires in the Mirror*. Plus there were hundreds of hours of other interviews that hadn't been used yet. Some of her material was written out and some was on tape. It was kind of a huge hodgepodge. Added to all this, they only gave us two and a half weeks to work; that was our deadline. So there was this huge push to edit down and select the best and most workable material. It was not an easy job, believe me. But it was fascinating.

How Anna Deavere Smith Works

The main thing Anna Deavere does when she's working with people is to wear a Walkman during her interviews with them. She tape-records everything. A lot of what we did was make an index card for each individual interview. Then we'd move the pieces around and figure out what structural questions were significant. Generally, people are going to say what they're going to say during the interviews, so we had to be selective as to what worked best for the interview, and what worked best for the play. We were kind of making up the rules as we went along.

Creating *Fires in the Mirror*

Fires in the Mirror is about the Crown Heights riots, both from the Jewish and the African-American perspectives. There were many questions during the interview about identity. Many of the questions focused on How do you define yourself? If someone asks you, "Who are you?" do you pull up race? Do you pull up gender? Do you pull up your job? Do you pull up where you live or who your parents are? Clearly everything exploded in Crown Heights around issues of difference. Then we had to deal with why those two communities found it necessary to define themselves in a way that was in direct opposition to each other.

Some Ideas about Solo Shows

My favorite way of working with a solo piece is starting from the seed of an idea with the actor-writer. As I mentioned, in this case, with Anna, she had already had a previous workshop, so it was a bit of a different process. One thing though, every solo show that I've worked on, the actor-writer is always hungry for input and dramaturgical assistance.

Ultimately one-person shows end up being a dialogue between the actor and the audience. The director stands in for the audience during rehearsal. You're the other half of the dialogue. During performance you actually become part of the audience and feel what they're feeling.

WORKING ON THE INTERVIEWS TO CREATE CHARACTERS

A lot of our discussions were about the reality of the piece. All of the decisions were about there being an actual person that was going to be portrayed by Anna on the stage. The editing decisions were all based on what was said during the interviews. Inevitably you have to change some of what they've said. But the secret is, you must remain truthful to the core of who they are. You really have to listen to what they're trying to say and see how it can filter into what the needs of your piece are.

There are a lot of interpretative decisions to be made that you have to tussle out in rehearsal. The hardest thing in that piece was that everybody was either happy or interested. Nobody was furious at all. Because Anna is African-American and a woman, we had to deal with things like how are you going to portray a Jewish male? How would you do his dialect without stereotyping him? When you're playing a man, what are you trying to hold on to as to what's masculine for that character, without being too overt?

BLOWN SIDEWAYS THROUGH LIFE

In *Blown Sideways through Life,* Claudia (Shear) and I developed the piece over about three years. There were many readings and small productions around the country prior to it settling in at The Cherry Lane Theater in New York. The piece started with an idea that Claudia had. She said, "There are things in my experience that I think could make a show. Would you help develop it with me?" She'd write material and then we'd talk. Then she'd write some more and we'd discuss that. It went on that way.

About two months into working this way, we decided she'd structure it around the jobs that she'd had. She'd bring material to me and we'd cull it, reshape it, and try it out over a couple of years. Claudia wrote every word, but structurally we developed together. When we first showed the piece, it was around thirty minutes. Eventually it ran sixty-seven minutes. At one point it went as long as an hour and a half, but we pulled it back down.

Because this was the first thing Claudia had written, it was at times like a roller coaster ride for her. Like "Wheeeee! What am I doing?! How do I write?!" She was figuring out where her voice was as she was writing. With Anna Deavere Smith, she had taught a lot and had written other plays, so the experience was quite different. Anna had a lot more self-awareness of what type of voice she would be writing in.

REHEARSAL PROCESS OF BOTH PIECES

Both pieces would have like a weaving in and out of rehearsing, followed by dramaturgical table work. We'd rehearse for about an hour and then we'd take a break back at the table where we'd edit down and reorganize. The way we rehearsed was, the actresses would get up and work on the text. There'd be some blocking, some physical stage work. They both worked on a set of some kind. We'd figure out what the physical life was and how the pacing would go. We'd work on how we were defining the characters at every given time. With Anna, there was a lot more character work. With Claudia, there was a dance element to the piece. Also in *Blown Sideways* there were these rapid fire lists that sometimes went on for a minute or two. Early on we decided that there would be like a stunt quality to these lists. They were going to go so fast and yet every element of the list had to be specific. That took a lot of memorizing and attaching specifics to them. We had to at first work very slowly. You'd look at each element of the list and ask, "How do you feel about it? What's the action attached to it?" Then we'd take it at one-half speed, then three-fourths speed, then all the way.

THE SIMILARITIES BETWEEN THE PIECES

There are certain similarities between both pieces. Both Anna's and Claudia's pieces have a play structure to them. In both cases the writer/primary creator is performing them. What I do is shape the production around the core of who both of them are and what their instincts are. In a regular play where you cast actors, I feel like they're working for me. The writer and I have created a framework that the actors are acting within. But in both of these two one-person shows, I'm creating a production that's faithful to the actors. I try to never hide or cover up what's particularly interesting about them. Both actresses are completely exposed in their shows. It's their instincts, they thought of it, they're doing it, it's their piece.

HIDING FROM THE AUDIENCE

One thing I find myself saying to one-person performers a lot in rehearsal is, "Don't hide from the audience." Especially with Claudia's piece which is all directly addressed to the audience, you cannot allow yourself to hide. There is a subtle but really important difference in those kinds of pieces, actually talking "at" the audience or talking "to" the audience. You certainly have to fake that in rehearsal because I, the director, am the only one who's there. But once you're in front of an audience you have to really talk to them. With Claudia, I remember, we constantly discussed at which point she would grab a specific person in the audience and talk to them. We also discussed when she would talk to the audience as a whole. At other times there would be a subtle kind of fourth wall up where she would do her own thing. It was very plotted out. People who come from an improv background especially like when people in the audience do stuff while they're looking at them, they'll respond to it.

MY FEELINGS ABOUT ONE-PERSON SHOWS

One of my favorite things about one-person shows is that how you work and what the show is, comes organically right out of the person who is performing in it. You have to reinvent a way of working each time for the person who is performing it. You have to find a vocabulary and method with each individual person. Whereas the director on prewritten plays has a more regulated way of working that generally works all the time.

DIRECTOR EGO GRATIFICATION

As far as director ego gratification, on one extreme end of the continuum is Shakespeare. New plays, with the writer in the room, are somewhere in the middle. And for me, in general, one-person plays are the most humbling experience for a director. Because if you direct very aggressively, kind of in your face, let the audience see your direction, I think you're making a terrible mistake.

THE DIRECTOR AND THE SOLO PERFORMER

About the relationship between the director and the solo performer, there is nobody throwing input into that process besides the two people working on the play. It's just the two of you in a very intense work situation. This really makes it a sort of marriage. It's very difficult from the outside to know how much the director did. Some directors do very little, justifiably, on a piece. In those cases, the actor uses the director like a friend who gives them feedback. But in other cases, the director is an absolutely central collaborator on the show.

TIPS ON WORKING ON SOLO SHOWS

In a one-person show, that one person is the center of everything. The tech that surrounds him should not overwhelm him. A lot of times, in blocking and transitions, I never want that person to go off stage if I can help it. I know that some actors do leave the stage during the performance, especially when playing multiple characters. But you always have to let the audience be in connection with that performer.

With Anna, one of the things we discovered in rehearsal was, anytime there was a transition time, say to change characters, it would kill it. We developed this thing where the last words from the previous piece and the first word of the next piece would be butted right up against each other. She would do whatever costume change or prop change, or go to a new area in the text. Everything was totally fluid; there was no edge. We had technical run-throughs to deal with these things. There was zero transition time allowed.

WHAT MAKES A GOOD ONE-PERSON SHOW

One of the thrilling things about one-person shows is that the good ones reinvent the form. The thrill of writing a one-person show is that you get to invent a new kind of theater for yourself. It's a great form for breaking the rules. Actors should ask themselves, "What does the show that's inside of me have that hasn't been seen before?" At some point in the evening I think every one-person show has to get really honest about who that person is. That is, what they think, what they feel, etc. Because you don't have dynamics between two characters in a one-person show, what you have is interesting, gutsy, honest acting. As a writer of a one-person show you have to conquer the problem of where variety is coming from. Because you're not going to have multiple voices or people, you have to take care of your audience in terms of creating differences for them to look at and feel. Arc is really important in one-person shows. You must have a beginning, middle, and end, and you have to arrive somewhere different from where you started. You have to set up a problem. And although you don't have to resolve it, you have to work through it. In a one-person show, directorially, less is generally more. The director must be really interested in the actor he will be working with because mostly your job is to serve him up to an audience. The director must bring that interest in the actor to the audience.

One of my favorite things about one-person shows is how much it empowers the actor. The actor is in control of his own destiny. But don't do it unless you really have something to talk about. One thing you should ask yourself is, "Is there something about what you've lived through that people need to hear?"

MARCIA JEAN KURTZ

Bob Newey Photos, NYC

Marcia Jean Kurtz directed the critically acclaimed productions *Time on Fire* by Evan Handler at Second Stage, and *Uncle Philip's Coat* by Matty Selman starring Larry Block at HB Playwrights Theater and The American Jewish Theater. As an actress, Ms. Kurtz received an Obie for her performance in Donald Margulies's *The Loman Family Picnic* at Manhattan Theater Club and an Obie and Drama Desk nomination for her performance in Martin Sherman's *When She Danced* at Playwrights Horizons. Ms. Kurtz was a member of Peter Brook's C.I.R.T., Jerome Robbins American Theater Lab, and Joseph Chaikin's Open Theater. She is currently a member of The Ensemble Studio Theater and The Lincoln Center Director's Lab Reviews.

- Lawrence Van Gelder, in the *New York Times,* said, "Here are three names: Larry Block, Matty Selman, and Marcia Jean Kurtz. They are the three talented principals behind *Uncle Philip's Coat,* the funny, insightful, and often touching play at the American Jewish Theater."
- Michael Feingold, in the *Village Voice,* said, "[under] Ms. Kurtz's self-effacing direction . . . the production elements are almost threadbare, the emotions are deep and the interplay of ironies and images are complex."

Interview with Marcia Jean Kurtz

MY FIRST ONE-PERSON SHOW

The first one-person play I directed was called *A Thread in My Head* by Frederica Meister. It was for E.S.T. (Ensemble Studio Theater) for the Octoberfest. I learned quite a bit while working on that piece.

It's interesting; I really don't see much difference between working on a solo piece and a regular play. The main thing is that the person who has written and is performing the piece is talented. The thing that matters most to me is that the text is wonderful. I noticed that Meister's piece had theatricality. There are some pieces that are only meant to be read, not to be acted out. You just know that those pieces don't have that vibrancy that you need to have someone standing in front of you and telling you something that has immediacy and vibrancy and imagery that you find with any playwright. If the dialogue within the monologue is something that needs to be told in the theater, it's there whether it's a monologue or any play.

ONE OF MY MAIN CONTRIBUTIONS

The thing that I have found is that I assist by being the editor and developer of the material. No one comes to me with a fully formed piece. Everyone comes to me with a bunch of material. It's very much a collaborative effort, making the piece a play. It's very much like being a literary manager, a dramaturge; at least that's my experience. The piece changes immensely during the rehearsal process.

If there's a sentence that absolutely defines the moment, reaches the audience, is active, that's what I'll want to keep. If there are ten other sentences after that that are boring, then, like any editor, you'll get rid of them. If there are parts of the story that aren't fleshed out, that you feel more needs to be told, you'll encourage the writer-actor to develop that.

If the piece needs to be more dramatic, or funnier, you'll point them in that direction. It's really very similar to what a book editor does when a novelist comes to him with a piece of writing.

HOW MY BACKGROUND HELPED ME WITH ONE-PERSON SHOWS

I think some of my instincts were developed just by being an actor and knowing what words you want to speak. If I pick up a script and start speaking the words, and I feel exhausted immediately, I know that it stinks. Yet I know if I'm having fun, if it engages me immediately, that I want to act it. I feel that a lot of my ideas come from being an actor, as well as being a great reader all my life.

Also, I studied dance and music. I was a choreographer at Julliard. All of those things come together when I work with someone. When I get bored, when I feel myself zoning out, I realize everyone else will too. Bottom line, you have to hook into what you feel is the story that you think this person wants to tell. It's a constant process. As the actor–writer comes to you each day and you rehearse, it's a constant chipping away, reshaping. You must get the writer to make the piece sharper, clearer. It's like Michelangelo chipping away at the marble until the sculpture reveals itself.

Quite often you see in one-person shows a lot of movement. There is a tendency in some directors to keep the actor moving, keep the eye going. I think that if the words are conveying the images clear enough, the audience will be immediately entranced because they will be transported by what the actor is talking about. When the moment cries out for something to be physicalized, the actor usually knows it. It's not something that I impose. People start moving when they start talking. From the little movements, the little human gestures that you see. Perhaps because of my work as a choreographer, I'm very aware of all the movements the actor is making. You can selectively make them more emphatic, larger, smaller, put them in to emphasize, etc. I think the performer shows you the way to what the physicalization of the piece will be.

How I Rehearse

I don't have a set way of working on a piece; I hope that I never do. At the first day of work, you just start with the first sentence of the piece and away you go. I personally like to work on a piece in sections. You watch what the actor is doing. And you say, "You know when you did that, that was great, let's remember that." It's like having a discussion with someone about the piece.

You don't want to go through the whole piece the first day; it's too exhausting. Since, for the most part, most solo writer-performers have said these words a hundred times while writing it, I don't think it's necessary to sit at a table and discover the text. I have to say that on all the pieces that I've worked on, the writing, doing, honing, and developing of it all seem to happen at the same time.

Lessons I've Learned

I've worked as an actor with Peter Brook, Joe Chaikin, and Jerome Robbins. I've worked with some wonderful people. I remember when Peter Brook walked into the first day of rehearsal. He had everything marked out like little toy soldiers where everyone would go. All of a sudden he looked up on the stage and said, "What's happening up there is much more interesting." He then threw out his blueprint. Most of the really good directors that I've worked with, I've noticed their inspiration came from who was up there in front of them, and what they were doing.

Knowing When It's Ready

How do you know when the piece is ready? When it has a great beginning, middle, and end, and I'm not falling asleep at any point. I want to be engaged, moved, from moment to moment. If I'm not, then something isn't working yet. Little by little you bring people in (whose opinion you trust) and you get their input. You can gauge what's working and what's not by just having a couple of smart friends come by and watch the piece.

WHAT WRITERS BRING TO THE TABLE

The wonderful thing is that every time a writer-actor brings you something new, you start fresh. You have a new world to explore. I try to find out how I can go there with them, to illuminate it. I think you really have to be pretty brave to trust the words, let the words do the job.

THE TRAP OF OVERPRODUCING

Overproducing a piece is the trap. There is that tendency to try to do too much with a piece. Both Evan Handler and Larry Block moved so well on stage. Their every gesture communicated so much. Even if stillness is at the center of the gesture, I'm always looking for the gesture of grace, the gesture of communication. It all comes down to one's style. I wouldn't want anything on the stage that wasn't eloquent.

Photo by Steven Adler

DAVID BAR KATZ

David Bar Katz co-created, produced, and was head writer of the Emmy-nominated Fox show *House of Buggin'.* He co-produced and wrote *The Pest* for Tristar Pictures, and he is the co-author of the book *Freak.* His novel *The Heaviest God* is published by Crown Publishers. Katz is the co-founder (with John Leguizamo) of Lower East Side Films. He is presently writing a screenplay of the science fiction novel *The Uplift War.* David Bar Katz both developed and directed the show *Freak.*

- Regarding *Freak,* Alexis Greene, in *In Theater Magazine,* said, "David Bar Katz keeps the pace energetic, and ultimately you are grateful that no scenic abracadabra competes with Leguizamo's blade-sharp comic timing."
- Clifford A. Ridley, in the *Philadelphia Inquirer,* said of *Freak,* "The show's director . . . tempers Leguizamo's natural ebullience with some welcome quiet moments. . . ."

Interview with David Bar Katz

HOW IT STARTED OUT

The way it started out was that John (Leguizamo) and I were writing *Freak* together; that's how the process began. John had actually wanted to do more of a stand-up show, as opposed to his previous one-man shows. He wanted to do like a Richard Pryor in concert kind of thing. So, at the beginning, we were writing almost stand-up type material. The rehearsal process and the writing process were like one and the same. Actually, even after we opened, we never stopped writing it, tweaking things.

HOW *FREAK* WAS DIFFERENT

Previously, on his other shows, John would come out in costume and do a character for about fifteen minutes. But, in this show, we weren't relying on costumes. In one five-minute scene of our show, John could be doing five or six characters, in the same costume, switching from character to character. What we worked on in rehearsals was the way the transitions would occur. They needed to be seamless.

HOW WE WORKED ON THE SHOW

The way we actually worked on a day-to-day basis was, we'd go over the script, discuss what the scene was about, the problems and the issues, and then would just start reading through it. John liked to put it on its feet as soon as possible. So much of his work was just getting comfortable with the physicality. We'd break down the scene into bits. We'd work on the comedy bits first and then on the dramatic bits. I'll give you an example of what I'm talking about. There was a scene where he's wrestling with his father, obviously playing both characters. We'd have to figure out the positioning of his body, just where his body is and how he can, in an instant, split to become his father's character. Stuff like that took a lot of work. Every now and then, just to get the right physical truth, I'd be a stand-in for his father in that scene.

We worked on *Freak* for a year and a half. We'd do readings all over the place, just to get audience reactions. My primary concern for the whole beginning part of the process was just the text, and working on the script. I knew that in relation to the staging of it, that would come later. What we were trying to do was something very difficult, a marriage of intense drama and broad comedy. We needed to find a balance there.

I met John five or six years ago. I was the publicist on John's show, *Mambo Mouth*. We became good friends. We eventually co-created the TV show *House of Buggin'*. We've been best friends, so working together was great, truly like a marriage, a good one. John and I think in similar ways, and we have a great trust.

My Contributions

John's initial agenda, as I mentioned, was that this was going to be a comedic show. One of my biggest contributions was helping him find the more dramatic levels in his material. Ostensibly, it was an autobiographical show about John, so it was at times like a process of psychoanalysis. There were places that John didn't want to go because they were too painful, and I had to keep pushing him, urging him on.

Characters came and went in the developmental process, and that would sometimes be difficult. Two characters were cut two days before we opened, and that was really tough. They were female characters, and his audiences love to see him do female characters. And although they were audience pleasers, they just didn't work in the play, structurally.

From the very beginning, our goal was to get to Broadway with the play. We didn't know if that was going to work out, but that was our goal. John had done two off-Broadway shows. So my view directorially was that everything had to be taken up a notch. John has a huge amount of energy; I felt we could use his energy and be as unconventional as we could on a Broadway stage. I felt we could utilize the space of a Broadway stage and fill it with John's tremendous energy in an organic way. We would even break the proscenium and have him climb the wall of the theater and go into the balcony. In another scene, he jumps back and forth covering the whole stage. We wanted it to have a sense of just John alone in the theater, playing. We wanted to break that wall between him and the audience.

The show was extremely tightly blocked. Because John is such a good actor, each audience thought they were seeing him move around at random, like for the first time. The hardest thing in the show was making it seem like it was improvised.

At first we just did readings at P.S. 122, then we workshopped the play as a work in progress at the Goodman Theater in Chicago, then we did six weeks at Theater In The Square In San Francisco, then six weeks at The Atlantic Theater in New York, and then ended up at the Cort Theater on Broadway.

The first reading was almost three-and-a-half hours long. It was epic. We certainly cut a lot of material. The feeling was never that we were trying to get it perfect, but rather how good could we get it. It was always an ongoing process. If the deadline wasn't for another year, we'd still be working on it. My feeling is, you can always find a better line, you can always set a scene slightly better. Since you're an artist and are constantly changing, so will your work. What you did six months ago isn't always the same truth that you might have today.

My Advice

My advice to your readers is that they must search themselves and find out what they're passionate about. Too many people decide to do one-person shows because they want to get an agent or jump-start a career. You must be brutally honest with yourself. What makes these kinds of shows interesting is the confessional quality they must have. You must be able to discern what is being just indulgent and what is of some interest to an audience. For any artist to be effective you must be aware that what is amusing or moving to yourself may not be the same for an audience.

The problem with so many actors is that because they're so taken with themselves, they have trouble discerning what is effective. That's one major reason why you must find a director whom you trust, who can help steer the way for you. That director must be able to comfortably tell the actor, what you're saying there isn't interesting, but what you said over there, is.

ANYTHING WORKS IF IT'S DONE WELL

I think anything can work in these kinds of shows if they're done well. I tried to do things in *Freak* that don't traditionally work in this kind of show. There was an aspect of like a Tennessee Williams sort of thing in our show. We'd go back into John's childhood, and suddenly John would become a narrator. In sort of a Proustian sort of way he'd take in the scene of his childhood while being John Leguizamo the narrator. It was a way of looking at the past and dreading it in some way and yet there was a longing for it. And all the time he was narrating this. I don't know if that all makes sense to you, but the way it played was very effective. Normally, a lot of directors would say, "Just do the scene." But we found this way of showing it much more effective. This type of narration would say, "This is who I am now, and this is what I'm feeling. Let me show you a little bit of what created who I am." If it feels fake, the audience will sense that.

WHAT *FREAK* WAS SAYING

In *Freak,* we (the audience) discover John's search for an individuation in his work, a search for his own identity. His work is about his own search in his life. I feel his earlier shows like *Mambo Mouth* were saying things like "I'm here, I'm Latin." I feel that was more like a statement. *Freak* is more of a textured work; it is more nuanced, which perhaps makes it more ambiguous as well.

ARTIST COLONIES WHERE YOU CAN DEVELOP YOUR SOLO SHOW

This section lists artist colonies where solo artists can escape to do their work in a tranquil and (usually) idyllic surrounding. Artists are offered a getaway opportunity where they can avoid life's pressures and annoyances. The fees for this dream working-vacation are small or non-existent, depending on the residency you apply to. Many of these residencies offer housing to artists in different disciplines. The deadline dates may change, so please always check with the residence that you're interested in prior to the deadline listed.

• **Apostle Islands National Lakeshore**
Route 1, Box 4, Bayfield, WI 54814, Tel. (715) 779-3397, FAX (715) 779-3049
Contact: Myra Dec

At this national park artist colony you can work on your solo material for two to three weeks between June and September. You are housed in a cabin on a beach near a forest. Be aware there is no electricity or running water, and you must provide your own food. They provide your transportation and housing. Primarily what this colony looks for are "writers with accomplishment, artistic integrity" who can appreciate the environment that they are housed in. You must complete an application, a sample of your work, a description of your solo material, and a résumé. The deadline is January 15. You'll hear from them in a couple of months.

• **Blue Mountain Center**
Box 109, Blue Mountain Lake, NY 12812, Tel. (518) 352-7391
Contact: Harriet Barlow

This residence is located in the Adirondacks. The available dates are between mid-June and October. Blue Mountain provides free room and board. Primarily, the colony looks for work that is appropriate for a general audience and deals with social issues. Send SASE for guidelines by February 1. You'll be notified by early April.

• Byrdcliffe Art Colony

The Woodstock Guild, 34 Tinker Street, Woodstock, NY 112498, Tel. (914) 679-2079, FAX (914) 679- 4529, E-mail: *wguild@ulster.net*, Web site: *www.ulster.net/-wguild*
Contact: Artists Residency Program

This colony offers a four-week residency between June and September at its three hundred acre colony in the Catskill Mountains. The residence is ninety miles from New York, near Woodstock. It offers private rooms and a space at Viletta Inn, a lovely mountain lodge. The residents provide their own food and cook in a common kitchen area. There is also a common living room where you can meet with some of the other artists. Aside from monologue writers, Byrdcliffe offers residencies to screenwriters, playwrights, librettists, and translators. To stay at Byrdcliffe, you must pay a $500 fee per session! To be eligible to stay here you must prove that you are a serious solo artist. Byrdcliffe looks for commitment to your work as a chief criterion. Send a self-addressed stamped envelope (SASE) for more information. You will be expected to send a completed application, a sample of your work, reviews of previous shows, a résumé, and at least two references plus a $5 fee. The deadline is April 1.

• Centrum Artist-In-Residency Program

Fort Worden State Park, Box 1158, Port Townsend, WA 98368, Tel. (360) 385-3102, FAX (360) 385-2470, Web site: *www.centrum.com*
Contact: Marlene Bennett

This residence offers a one-month stay between September and May. The residence is located on the 440-acre Fort Worden State Park. It offers self-contained cabins plus a separate studio space to write in. There is no charge for facilities. The program looks for writers who show a clear sense of direction in their work and have some accomplishments. You are required to complete an application and a description of your project, along with a résumé and a sample of your work. The deadline is October 1, with notification by mid-November.

• The Gell Writers Center

c/o Writers and Books, 740 University Avenue, Rochester, NY 14607, Tel. (716) 473-2590, FAX (716) 729-0982
Contact: Joseph Flaherty

This residence offers two private bedrooms, year round, in a house surrounded by twenty-three acres of forest. It occasionally offers creative writing workshops for an additional fee. Residents pay $35 per day. The Center requests that you call or write for an application. The deadline for this residence is ongoing.

• Hedgebrook

2197 East Millman Road, Langley, WA 98260, Tel. (360) 321-4786, FAX (360) 321-4786
Contact: Linda Bowers

This residence is for women of different cultural backgrounds. Hedgebrook offers cottages on Whidbey Island, surrounded by a wooded area. Room and board is free. Any woman writer is invited to apply. Send a SASE for application. Hedgebrook requests that you return the application with a work sample, a description of the solo material that you're working on, and a $15 fee. If you'd like to stay there in the winter or spring, submit the required material by October 1. If you'd like to stay there in the summer or fall, contact the colony by April 1. Generally, you'll be notified in a couple of months.

- **Isle Royal National Park Artist-In-Residence**
  800 East Lakeshore Drive, Houghton, MI 49931, Tel. (906) 482-8753, FAX (906) 482-8753,
  Web site: *www.nps.gov/isro/*
  Contact: Greg Blust

This residence offers a two- to three-week stay between June to September, in a cabin on a very quiet island near Lake Superior. Only one artist is housed at a time. There is no electricity, and you must provide your own food. The program expects the artist selected to be able to exist in this natural environment and to donate time for work in the park. Isle Royal National Park requests that you complete an application, include a description of your project, your résumé, and a sample of a project that you've worked on. The deadline for this residence is February, and you're notified by mid-April.

- **New York Mills Arts Retreat**
  24 North Main Avenue, Box 246, New York Mills, MN 56567, Tel. (218) 385-3339,
  FAX (218) 385-3366, E-mail: *nymills@uslink.net*
  Contact: Kent Scheer

This residence operates year round. Housing is offered to one artist at a time for a two- to four-week stay. The residence is part of a small farming community. There is a fee of $750 for a two-week stay and $1,500 for a four-week stay. The artist is expected to work in the community for at least eight hours per week during his stay. Those interested must complete an application, send a sample of their work, and give a description of the project they plan to work on. They should also include two letters of recommendation. The deadlines for this residence are October 1 and April 1. You'll hear from the retreat about eight weeks after the deadline.

- **Studio for Creative Inquiry**
  Carnegie Mellon University, College of Fine Arts, Pittsburgh, PA 15213-3890,
  Tel. (412) 268-3454, FAX (412) 268-2829
  Contact: Marge Myers

This residence offers two different types of residencies, year round. The first, the shorter one, is for two weeks to three months. The longer residency is from six months to three years. A studio facility and any necessary equipment are provided in Carnegie Mellon's College of Fine Arts building. The College assists artists in finding housing. A stipend is provided. The college requests that you send a work sample and résumé. The deadline for this residence is open. Generally you'll hear from the studio in a couple of months.

- **Virginia Center for the Creative Arts**
  Box VCCA, Mt. San Angelo, Sweet Briar, VA 24595, Tel. (804) 846-7236, FAX (804) 946-7239,
  E-mail: *vcca@vcca.com*
  Contact: The Director

This year round residency offers housing from two weeks to two months at a 450-acre estate in the Blue Ridge Mountains. The resident pays $30 a day for room and board (if they can afford it). The Virginia Center requests that you fill out their application and return it with a sample of your work, two letters of recommendation, and a copy of your résumé. The center bases its decision on your past success or potential and promise. The deadline for the January to April residency is September 15. The deadline for the May to August residency is January 15. The deadline for the September to December residency is May 15. Generally you'll hear from the center in a couple of months.

APPENDIX B

THEATERS THAT ACCEPT SOLO MATERIAL

This appendix includes theaters to which you can submit your material. Be selective about where you send your work. It's important to read the general information about the theater. If they're interested in solo material that is unusual or surreal, don't send your naturalistic monologue. If they say not to send unsolicited material, don't.

Always include a letter of inquiry and a synopsis of the monologue when writing to potential theaters.

• **Actors' and Playwrights' Initiative**
API Theater, Box 50051, Kalamazoo, MI 49005-0051, Tel. (616) 343-8310, FAX (616) 343-8310
Contact: Robert C. Walker

Unsolicited material is not accepted. The theater only wants to hear from writers living in Illinois, Indiana, Michigan, Ohio, Wisconsin, and Ontario. The theater will, however, accept a synopsis of your show. Also include a résumé and a letter of inquiry with a SASE for response. Actors' and Playwright's Initiative is particularly interested in gay material and provocative social and political work. The best time to submit is May through October. Generally, you'll get a response in two to six months. The remuneration is negotiable.

• **The Actors Theater**
P.O. Box 780, Talent, OR 97540-0780, Tel. (541) 535-5250
Contact: Chris Sackett

This is a community, non-professional theater. The theater requests that you send a query, synopsis with about ten pages of dialogue from your show, a résumé, and a SASE. Please do not send unsolicited scripts or tapes of your show. The Actors Theater creates tours of solo shows, and likes the unusual and bizarre as well as family fare. You may have to wait a month or two for a response.

• Actors Theater of Louisville
316 West Main Street, Louisville, KY 40202-4218, Tel. (502) 584-1265, FAX (502) 561-3300,
E-mail: *actors@aye.net*
Contact: Michael Bigelow Dixon or Amy Wegener

Unsolicited videotapes/scripts are accepted for their Flying Solo and Friends Festival, an important venue for solo artists. Actors Theater reads about twenty-five hundred scripts a year and produces twenty to forty (this doesn't include the Flying Solo Festival). You can submit your material year round, but check when their deadlines are for the solo festivals. This year it's December 31.

• American Music Theater Festival
123 Broad Street, 18th floor, Philadelphia, PA 19109, Tel. (215) 893-1570 or (800) 318-AMTF,
FAX (215) 893-1570
Contact: David McCane

Do not send unsolicited material, as it is not accepted; rather, only submissions through agents or individual artists are, and new and experimental work is preferred. Generally, your agent will hear from American Music Theater Festival in about four months.

• Arena Stage
1101 6th Street SW, Washington, DC 20024, Tel. (202) 554-9066, FAX (202) 488-4056
Contact: Cathy Madison

Unsolicited material is not accepted, only a synopsis of your material, bio, and letter of inquiry. Arena Stage is specifically interested in material from women, writers of color, disabled, and other nonmainstream artists. If you send a letter, the theater will respond almost immediately. Scripts can take up to six months for a response. The best time to contact Arena is in the late summer to early fall.

• ART Station
Box 1998, Stone Mountain, GA 30086, Tel. (770) 469-1105, FAX (770) 469-0355,
E-mail: *artstation@mindspring.com*
Contact: Jon Goldstein

Unsolicited material is accepted. ART prefers that your show has not been professionally produced before. ART is especially looking for material from southern artists or plays with southern themes. The best time to contact the theater is between June and December. It generally takes about two months for the theater to respond.

• Asolo Theater Company
Asolo Center for the Performing Arts, 5555 North Tamiami Trail, Sarasota, FL 34243,
Tel. (941) 351-9010, FAX (941) 351-5796, E-mail: *brodge@worldnet.att.net*
Contact: Bruce E. Rogers

Unsolicited material is not accepted. Asolo does accept a one-page synopsis of your piece and a letter of inquiry. Don't forget the SASE for a response. The best time to submit material is June through August. Generally, you'll hear back in two to six months. The remuneration is negotiable.

- **Attic Theater Center**
  6562½ Santa Monica Blvd., Hollywood, CA 90038, Tel. (213) 469-3786, FAX (213) 463-9571
  Contact: Gil Roscoe

  Unsolicited material is not accepted, but you can send a synopsis of your work with your résumé and a letter of inquiry (with a SASE) for a response. Minority subjects are preferred. This is a ninety-nine–seat house. You can submit your material all year round. You should hear from Attic in a few months.

- **Bailiwick Repertory**
  1229 West Belmont, Chicago, IL 60657-3205, Tel. (773) 883-1090
  Contact: David Zak

  Send a SASE for guidelines for submissions. Bailiwick likes women's, gay, deaf, and political material. You can submit all year round. It can take up to a year for the theater to respond. You'll hear from Bailiwick in about nine months.

- **Bay Street Theater**
  Box 810, Sag Harbor, NY 11963, Tel. (516) 725-0818, FAX (516) 628-0906, Web site: *www.baystreet.org*
  Contact: Mia Emlen Grosjean

  No unsolicited material accepted, only agent submissions. Bay Street Theater likes innovative material that is interesting as well as entertaining. Your agent can submit year round, but the theater prefers submissions in June through January. Generally, you'll hear back from them in three to six months.

- **Berkshire Theater Festival**
  Box 797, Stockbridge, MA 01262, Tel. (413) 298-5536, FAX (413) 298-3368,
  E-mail: *info@berkshiretheater.org*, Web site: *www.berkshiretheater.org*
  Contact: John Unruh

  Agent submissions only. Provocative, cutting edge material is preferred. The best time for contact is October through December. Generally, you'll hear from them in about three months.

- **Bristol Riverside Theater**
  Box 1250, Bristol, PA 19007, Tel. (215) 785-6664, FAX (215) 785-2762
  Contact: David J. Abers

  Unsolicited material is accepted. The theater likes innovative, cutting edge material. You should contact them in January. If you send a letter, you'll hear from Bristol in four to six months. If you send your material, expect a response in six to eighteen months.

- **Carmel Performing Arts Festival**
  Box 221473, Carmel, CA 93922, Tel. (408) 644-8383, FAX (408) 647-4531, E-mail: *rmckee@mbay.net*,
  Web site: *www.carmelfest.org*
  Contact: Robin McKee

  Carmel Performing Arts Festival requests that you are referred to it by a professional. The best submission time is March. Generally, you'll hear from them in four to five months.

- **Cleveland Public Theater**
  6415 Detroit Avenue, Cleveland, OH 44102-3011, Tel. (216) 631-2727, FAX (216) 631-2575,
  E-mail: *cpt@en.com*
  Contact: James A. Levin

Cleveland Public Theater prefers a letter of inquiry and a synopsis of your solo material. If you want, you may also send a ten-page sample of your work. The theater is adventurous in its taste; it prefers nothing too mainstream. If your work is experimental or provocative, contact it. It also prefers to be contacted by gay people, people of color, and women. Contact Cleveland Public Theater from February through October. For certain festivals a $10 submission fee is charged. You'll hear back in about six weeks (letter) to nine months (sent material).

• A Contemporary Theater

The Eagles Building, 700 Union Street, Seattle, WA 98101-2330, Tel. (206) 292-7660, FAX (206) 292-7660
Contact: Leslie Swackhamer

A Contemporary Theater requests that you *do not* send unsolicited material. It will, however, accept a synopsis of solo shows, with ten pages of dialogue, from northwest writers only. The material should be current, political, and psychological. The best time to contact A Contemporary Theater is September through April. Response time is three to six months. The theater pays royalties for accepted pieces.

• Edyvean Repertory Theater

1400 East Hanna Avenue, Indianapolis, IN 46227, Tel. (317) 927-8052, FAX (317) 927-8059, E-mail: *ert@indy.net,* Web site: *www.edyvean.org*
Contact: Karla Ries

Edyvean Repertory Theater accepts unsolicited material. You can submit your material year round. Generally, you'll get a response in six months.

• Emelin Theater for the Performing Arts

Library Lane, Mamaroneck, NY 10543, Tel. (914) 698-3045
Contact: David Watson

Unsolicited material is accepted, but only with a professional recommendation. Agent submissions are preferred. You should include your video when submitting. The theater looks for solo pieces that have "theatricality." Emelin accepts submissions year round. You'll hear back in about two months.

• The Ensemble Theater

3535 Main Street, Houston, TX 77002-9529, Tel. (713) 520-0055, FAX (713) 520-1269
Contact: Ellen J. Morris

Unsolicited material is accepted. The Ensemble is especially looking for African-American material. The best time to contact Ensemble is in October through April. You'll get a response in about two to three months.

• GALA Hispanic Theater

Box 43209, Washington, DC 20010, Tel. (202) 234-7174, FAX (202) 302-5041,
Contact: Hugo J. Medrano

Unsolicited material is accepted but a synopsis and letter of inquiry is preferred. GALA is especially interested in hearing from Hispanic-Americans (writing either in English or Spanish), solo pieces by Spanish writer-actors, as well as work that reflects the Hispanic-American experience. The best time to contact GALA is April/May. You'll hear back in about a month (for a letter) and in about eight months if you send your material.

- **Gary Young Mime Theater**
23724 Park Madrid, Calabasas, CA 91302, Tel. (202) 234-7174, FAX (202) 332-1247,
E-mail: *gyoung6364@aol.com*
Contact: Gary Young

The Gary Young Mime Theater is actively seeking comic monologues (physical theater). Query letters are accepted with a dialogue sample from your monologue. Include your résumé. You'll get a response in two to four months. The remuneration varies.

- **Hofstra U.S.A. Productions**
Hofstra Cultural Center, 109 Hofstra University, Hempstead, NY 11550-1090, Tel. (516) 463-5569
Contact: Bob Spiotto

Hofstra is seeking one-person shows. You can send a query/synopsis along with your résumé and a SASE. You can submit year round. Expect to get a response in two to four weeks. The remuneration is negotiable.

- **John Drew Theater**
158 Main Street, East Hampton, NY 11937, Tel. (516) 324-0806, FAX (516) 324-2722
Contact: Bridget Blachere

Unsolicited material is not accepted. You can send a one-page synopsis of your piece. You can contact John Drew all year round. Generally, you'll hear back in three months. Remuneration is negotiable.

- **La Mama Experimental Theater Club**
74A East 4th Street, New York, NY 10003, Tel. (212) 254-6468, FAX (212) 254-7597
Contact: Meryl Vladmir

La Mama accepts unsolicited videos of your show (with synopsis). It does, however, prefer a professional recommendation. As the name implies, La Mama prefers experimental, surreal, innovative work. The theater has a "One Night Stand" series where writers can perform their own work. You can contact La Mama year round. You'll hear from them in two to six months.

- **New York Theater Workshop**
79 East 4th Street, New York, NY 10003, Tel. (212) 780-9037
Contact: Mandy Mishell Hackett

New York Theater Workshop doesn't accept unsolicited material. Send a query letter and a résumé. New York Theater Workshop looks for socially relevant material and minority issues. The theater is especially interested in language and form. New York Theater Workshop looks for long-term collaborative relationships. Proposals for performance projects are accepted. The best time to submit is in the fall or spring. You'll get a response in about six months.

- **Offstage Theater**
P.O. Box 131, Charlottesville, VA 22902, Tel. (804) 961-8551, E-mail: *ldg2h@virginia.edu*
Contact: William Rough

This is a semi-professional, not-for-profit theater. It accepts unsolicited material with a query letter, synopsis, and SASE. Offstage seeks monologues, especially ones that can be performed in bars, fitness centers, galleries, and so on for site-specific staging. It prefers that the material be lightweight and simple. You'll hear from Offstage in one to six months.

• Primary Stages Company
584 9th Avenue, New York, NY 10036, Tel. (212) 333-7471, FAX (212) 333-2025
Contact: Tricia McDermott

Primary Stages does not accept unsolicited material. It prefers a ten-page dialogue sample, résumé, and letter of inquiry (with SASE). You can submit anytime, but from September to June is preferable. The theater is closed July through August. You'll hear from Primary Stages in a few months.

• Society Hill Playhouse
507 East 8th Street, Philadelphia, PA, 19147, Tel. (215) 923-0210, FAX (215) 923-1789
Contact: Walter Vail

This theater is especially interested in one-person shows. You can send a query letter with a synopsis of your piece (with a SASE). Material is accepted only by agent submission or through a recommendation. You'll hear from Society Hill in about one to six months.

• Timothy Childs Theatricals
1560 Broadway, Suite 1100, New York, NY 10036, Tel. (212) 840-3900, FAX (212) 840-1973,
E-mail: *childstim@aol.com*
Contact: Timothy Childs

This production company accepts agent submissions only. Timothy Childs is actively looking for one-person shows for Broadway.

• The Wooden O Drama Studio
2207 Federal Avenue, Los Angeles, CA 90064, Tel. (310) 477-2199
Contact: The Producing Director

This theater accepts unsolicited material. It requests that you send a query, a synopsis of your show, and a SASE. Wooden O particularly is looking for material that deals with the human condition.

• Woolly Mammoth Theater
1401 Church Street NW, Washington, DC 20005, Tel. (202) 234-6130, FAX (202) 667-0904,
E-mail: *gaowooly@aol.com*
Contact: Gary Oiler

Unsolicited material is accepted. Woolly Mammoth is especially looking for unusual, offbeat, and surreal material. You can submit all year round. Expect to hear back in four to six months. The remuneration is negotiable.

Publishers
of Solo Material

Having your solo piece published is certainly one way to feel validated and get some type of recognition for your work. But before you submit your manuscript to anyone, it is in your best interest to find out something about the publisher to whom you're submitting your manuscript. You'll want to be sure that your work will be presented in the best way. You should feel confident that you are dealing with a reputable and honest publisher.

Contact:

- **The Author's Guild**
  330 West 42nd Street, New York, NY 10036, Tel. (212) 563-5904

- **The Council of Literary Magazines and Presses**
  154 Christopher Street, Suite 3C, New York, NY 10014-2839, Tel. (212) 741-9110

  Request the Directory of Literary Magazines. It costs $12.95 plus $3.05 for first-class postage. This publication lists hundreds of magazines.

- **The Dramatists Guild**
  1501 Broadway, Suite 701, New York, NY 10036, Tel. (212) 398-9366

- **The International Directory of Little Magazines and Small Presses**
  Dustbooks, Box 100, Paradise, CA 95967, Tel. (530) 877-6110

  This periodical costs $32.95 paper, $47.95 cloth, plus $6.00 for shipping and handling.

Another thing you can do is write to some of the publishers that are listed below and ask them for sample copies or catalogues:

- **Alabama Literary Review**
253 Smith Hall, Troy State University, Troy, AL 36082, Tel. (334) 670-3307, FAX (334) 670-3519
Contact: Theron Montgomery

This is an annual literary journal. It accepts unsolicited manuscripts, but prefers a query letter, synopsis of your monologue, and a professional recommendation. Alabama Literary Review publishes work that is less than fifty pages (but less than thirty is preferred). The playwrights receive three complimentary copies. When the funds are available, the journal pays $5 to $10 per page. Generally, you'll hear back in two weeks (query letter) to three months (script).

- **Amelia Magazine**
329 E Street, Bakersfield, CA 93304, Tel. (805) 323-4064, E-mail: *amelia@lightspeed.ent*
Contact: Frederick A. Raborg, Jr.

The winner of the Frank McClure One-Act Play festival is published in this magazine. Send your monologue play plus any information about past productions. Include a $15 fee. The deadline is usually May of each year, but check to make sure.

- **Aran Press**
1320 South 3rd Street, Louisville, KY 40208-2306, Tel. (502) 636-0115
Contact: Tom Eagen

Aran Press accepts unsolicited material, but prefers a letter of inquiry and SASE. Generally Aran looks for material that is appropriate for summer stock, community theaters, colleges and universities, and dinner theater. More specifically, it looks for works that are "funny comedies or top-notch dramas." If your material is accepted, the remuneration is 10 percent for book royalty, 50 percent for production royalty. Be aware that the Press expects you to contribute to the publishing costs (about $150) and prefers a professional production first (before submission). Generally, you'll hear from Aran Press in about two weeks.

- **The Bellingham Review**
The Signpost Press, Mall Stop 9053, Western Washington University, Bellingham, WA 98225,
Web site: *www.wwu.edu/-bhreview*   *Contact:* Robin Henley

Bellingham is a biannual small press periodical. No solo pieces should be over ten thousand words. The piece must be unpublished, but Bellingham is not opposed to simultaneous submissions. Unsolicited material is accepted, but you should only submit to them from September 1 through May 1. The remuneration is one complimentary copy and a one-year subscription. You'll get a response in a few months.

- **Contemporary Drama Service**
Meriwether Publishing, Ltd., 885 Elkton Drive, Colorado Springs, CO 80907, Tel. (719) 594-4422,
FAX (719) 594-9916   *Contact:* Arthur L. Zapel

Unsolicited material is accepted. Send $2 for sample catalogue and guidelines. Meriwether publishes books of original monologues. It publishes material that is suitable for high schools, teenagers, the college market, church groups, and community theaters. It is especially interested in authors with name recognition. Generally, you'll hear from Contemporary in about two months. The remuneration is royalty up to buy-out figure. Be aware that the publisher holds the copyright.

- **Crazy Quilt Quarterly**
Box 632729, San Diego, CA 92163-2729   *Contact:* Marsh Cassady

This is a quarterly literary journal. Crazy Quilt Quarterly publishes solo pieces that are not more than thirty pages long and "not pornography." Its readership consists of writers, agents, and libraries. Remuneration is two complimentary copies of the publication. You'll hear from Crazy Quilt in two weeks to three months.

- **Descant**
Box 314 Station P, Toronto, Ontario M5S 258 Canada, Tel. (416) 593-2557   *Contact:* Mary Myers

This is a quarterly literary magazine. It accepts unsolicited material. Descant is looking for performance arts texts (unpublished) of any form or type. The remuneration is a $100 honorarium and one complimentary copy of the magazine. The response time is about six months.

- **The Dramatic Publishing Company**
311 Washington Street, Box 129, Woodstock, IL 60098, Tel. (815) 338-7170, FAX (815) 338-8981, E-mail: *75712.3621@compuserve.com,* Web site: *www.dramaticpublishing.com*
Contact: Linda Habjan

Dramatic Publishing accepts unsolicited material. It publishes books of monologues and prefers works that have been produced. The readership is stock, amateur market, professional, community, and college. The remuneration is the standard royalty plus ten complimentary copies. Response time is two to four months.

- **Earth's Daughters**
Box 41, Central Park Station, Buffalo, New York 14215, Tel. (716) 837-7778

This is a feminist literary and art periodical published three times a year. It accepts unsolicited material with a SASE. The remuneration is two complimentary copies. Response time is about two months.

- **Encore Performance Publishing**
Box 692, Orem, UT 84057, Tel. (801) 225-0605   *Contact:* Michael C. Perry

Encore doesn't accept unsolicited material. Send a synopsis and production information about your piece, with a letter of inquiry. The best time to make contact is May–August. You'll hear back in a few weeks to a few months. Encore publishes ten to thirty plays a year. You should have had at least two amateur or professional productions. The publisher especially looks for family, religious, and holiday material. The remuneration is 10 percent for book royalty and ten complimentary copies. Encore prefers that your material has no profanity in it and that it doesn't misuse the name of God. It does, however, like subjects of a controversial nature (if handled with discretion).

- **Kalliope, a Journal of Women's Literature and Art**
Florida Community College, 3939 Roosevelt Boulevard, Jacksonville, FL 32205
Contact: Mary Sue Koeppel

This journal, published three times a year, looks for work by women. It does accept unsolicited material. Kalliope requests that your solo work be less than twenty-five pages long and not of an erotic nature. It wants material that is original, not trite. Remuneration is three free copies or a free one-year subscription. It will take three to six months to get a response to your submission.

• The Kenyon Review
Kenyon College, Gambier, OH 43022, Tel. (740) 427-5202, FAX (740) 427-5417,
E-mail: *kenyonreview@kenyon.edu*   *Contact:* David H. Lynn

This literary journal generally publishes about two plays (including solo works) per year. It is published four times a year. It accepts unsolicited material as long as it's unpublished and unproduced and a maximum of thirty pages. They will either pay you with a cash payment or two complimentary copies. Submit from September through April (with SASE). Generally you'll get a response in about three months.

• Lamia Ink!
Box 202, Prince Street Station, New York, NY 10012
Contact: Cortland Jessup

This magazine looks for short monologues and especially performance art pieces. It is published three times a year. It prefers that the material not exceed five pages, and accepts unsolicited material with a SASE. If your material is accepted, you'll get four free copies.

• Players Press
Box 1132, Studio City, CA 91614-0132, Tel. (818) 789-4980
Contact: Robert W. Gordon

This company publishes all sorts of theater related books. The readership is worldwide (with special interests in theater related material). It accepts unsolicited submissions with verification that your work was produced. Send a copy of your material with a résumé and SASE. It may take up to six months to hear from Players Press.

• Provincetown Arts/Provincetown Art Press
650 Commercial Street, Provincetown, MA 02657, Tel. (508) 487-3167, FAX (508) 487-8634,
E-mail: *press@capecodaccess.com*
Contact: Christopher Busa

Provincetown Art Press generally likes to work with writers who are out at Cape Cod at some point during the year. The Press says that readership exceeds thirty-five thousand, and it accepts unsolicited material. Payment ranges from $50–$300 for accepted material. The company is looking for all sorts of solo pieces.

• Publish-on-Demand Script Service
Blizzard Publishing, 73 Furby Street, Winnipeg, Canada MB R3C 2A2, Tel. (204) 775-2923 or
(800) 694-9256, FAX (204) 775-2947   *Contact:* David Fuller

This company accepts unsolicited monologues. You should send for its guidelines and submission forms. It publishes more than sixty pieces a year in a chapbook format. It requires that your work have been previously produced. The remuneration is 10 percent book royalty. Generally, you'll hear back in four to six months.

• Smith and Kraus
Box 127, Lyme, NH 03768, Tel. (603) 643-6431, FAX (603) 643-1831, E-mail: *sandk@sover.net*
Contact: Marisa Smith

This small publishing company publishes monologue books and other solo work. It will give you ten complimentary copies or an agreed upon royalty. It doesn't accept unsolicited material. Send a letter of inquiry regarding your work. You'll hear back in a few months. The best time to contact Smith and Kraus is mid-August.

PLAYWRITING COMPETITIONS THAT ACCEPT SOLO MATERIAL

Another potential source for income from and exposure for your monologue play is to enter it into playwriting competitions. These nationally held contests offer cash prizes and, in some cases, production opportunities to winners. A few things to keep in mind before entering your monologue/solo work:

- If a competition requests that you send for guidelines, do so. These guidelines give specific instructions for that particular contest. In some cases, they even request that you fill out an application form to send with your material.

- One smart piece of advice: Send your material in earlier rather than close to the deadline. Most of us wait until the last minute to send things. In this case, that choice could work to your disadvantage. If you send the material earlier, your chances of getting a good read of your material are better. By deadline time, the judges are quite often exhausted and just want to get through the material as fast as they can.

- Be aware of the entrance fees of some of the competitions. Supposedly, these are to aid in the cost of running the competition. Always send a SASE with your material.

• Annual Blank Theater Company Young Playwrights Festival

1301 Lucile Avenue, Los Angeles, CA 90026, Tel. (213) 662-7234, FAX (213) 661-3903,
E-mail: *btc@primenet.com,* Web site: *www.prmwnnwt.com/-portal/*
Contact: April Dawn

To enter this competition, you must be nineteen years old or younger. Send your mono-
logue/solo material with a cover sheet that has your name, address, phone number, birth date,
and the school you attend. The deadline is April. The nine winners of this competition are given
a production as a prize. Winners are notified a month later. Note: Do not send a SASE. Scripts
will not be returned.

• Center Theater International Playwriting Competition

1346 West Devon Avenue, Chicago, IL 60660, Tel. (312) 508-0220   *Contact:* Dale Calandra

This competition offers a $300 award to the winner. Your solo material cannot have been pub-
lished, previously produced, or presently under option. The Center requests that you send a
SASE for guidelines and application form. Just so that you know, there is a $15 fee to enter this
competition, and your script will not be returned. The deadline has not been announced yet.
Last year it was in August.

• The Cunnigham Prize Theater School

DePaul University, 2135 North Kenmore, Chicago, IL 60614-4111, Tel. (773) 325-8938,
FAX (773) 325-7920, E-mail: *lgoetsch@wppost.depaul.edu,*
Web site: *http://theaterschool.depaul.edu/prize.htm*   *Contact:* Lara Goestsch

The prize given to the winner of this competition is $5,000! The contest requests that you live
in the Chicago area to apply (within one hundred miles of downtown Chicago). The competition requests that you send for specific guidelines. The kind of work that is sought "affirms the
centrality of religion, broadly defined, and the human quest for meaning, truth, and community." The deadline is December. You'll be notified by March of the next year.

• Dramarama Playwright's Center of San Francisco

P.O. Box 460466, San Francisco, CA 94146-0466, Tel. (415) 626-4603, E-mail: *playctrsf@aol.com*
Contact: Sheppard Kominars

There is a $25 entry fee. The award is $500. Your entry should not have been published or previously produced (except in a workshop production). They request that you send a SASE for
guidelines. The deadline is March 15, but Dramarama requests that you don't enter before
January l.

• Henrico Theater Company One-Act Playwriting Competition

County of Henrico, Division of Recreation and Parks, P.O. Box 27032, Richmond, VA 23273,
Tel. (804) 672-5100, FAX (804) 672-5284   *Contact:* J. Larkin Brown

The winner of this competition receives $250. The two runners up are awarded $250 each. The
theater requests that your solo piece be unproduced and unpublished. Send SASE for guidelines. The deadline is July 1. You'll be notified by December 31.

• HRC'S Annual Playwriting Competition

Hudson River Classic's Inc., P.O. Box 940, Hudson, NY 12534, Tel. (518) 828-1329
Contact: W. Keith Hedrick

The prize for this play is $500 plus a staged reading of your monologue. HRC will also provide
travel and accommodations to the winner. To enter this competition you must live in New York

State. Your work must be unpublished and cannot exceed ninety minutes. There is a $5 fee to enter this competition. Send your material and a SASE. The deadline is June 1, but HRC requests that you don't submit before March 1. You'll be notified by mid-November.

- **Inner City Cultural Center Competition**
1605 North Ivar Avenue, Los Angeles, CA 90028, Tel. (213) 962-2102, FAX (213) 386-9017
Contact: C. Bernard Jackson

There is a $45 entry fee! This contest offers a $1,000 prize to the winner. The second prize is $500, and the third prize is $250. The competition also offers internships with major Hollywood studios to the winners. Your play should be ready and fully mounted. Inner City Cultural Competition will provide the entire technical backup to produce it (lighting, crew, sound, etc.). Your piece cannot exceed forty minutes! Send SASE for guidelines. The deadline is March. Response time is a couple of months.

- **Jane Chambers Playwriting Award**
200 North Michigan Avenue, Suite 300, Chicago, IL 60601, Tel. (513) 873- 4128, FAX (513) 873-8787, E-mail: *mdonahoe@desire.wright.edu*
Contact: Mary Donahoe

This competition offers a $1,000 first prize with a possible staged reading of your work. There is also a student award of $250 and five finalists and fifteen honorable mentions. The contest prefers that those submitting have works that experiment with form. The authors must be women! Works that " reflect a feminist perspective" are sought. Send a SASE for guidelines. If you have a videotape recording of your piece, send it with your application. The deadline is February 15. You'll be notified by June 15.

- **Jewel Box Theater Playwriting Competition**
3700 North Walker, Oklahoma City, OK 73118, Tel. (405) 521-1786
Contact: Charles Tweed

The prize is $500. Send a SASE for guidelines. Jewel Box looks for "characterization" in your work. There is a $5 entrance fee. The deadline is January 15. The winner is announced in May.

- **Marvin Taylor Playwriting Contest**
Sierra Repertory Theater, P.O. Box 3030, Sonora, CA 95370, Tel. (209) 532-3120, FAX (209) 532-7270
Contact: Dennis Jones

The award for this competition is $500 with the chance of a possible production. Your work must be unpublished and you cannot have had more than two productions. Sierra Repertory requests that you send a copy of your monologue with a SASE. The deadline is August 31, with winners announced in March of the next year.

- **Mildred and Albert Panowski Playwriting Award**
Forest A. Roberts Theater, Northern Michigan University, Marquette, MI 49855, Tel. (906) 227-2553, FAX (906) 227-2567
Contact: James A. Panowski

The award for this competition is $2000! The competition also provides transportation and room and board for a one-week residency for a production of your work. Winners will also be entered in the Kennedy Center American College Theater Festival (if you're eligible). Your play must be unpublished and previously unproduced. Send for guidelines and entry form (with SASE). The deadline is November 21. You'll hear back by April of the next year.

• The Mill Mountain Theater New Play Competition

The Norfolk Southern Festival of New Works, 1 Market Square SE, 2nd floor, Roanoke, VA 24011-1437, Tel. (540) 342-5730, FAX (540) 342-5745, E-mail: *mmtmail@intrlink.com*, Web site: *www.intrlink.com/mmy*   *Contact:* Jack Parrish

The remuneration is $1000. Mill Mountain also may do a staged reading of your monologue and a possible production. They'd provide travel and housing accommodations. Your piece must be unpublished and previously unproduced. Send SASE for guidelines. Your piece must be either submitted by an agent or with a professional recommendation. The deadline is January 1. You'll hear back by August. Please do not submit your work before October 1.

• Theodore Ward Prize for African-American Playwrights

Columbia College Chicago, Theater, Music Center, 72 East 11th Street, Chicago, IL 60605, Tel. (312) 344-6136, FAX (312) 663-9591, E-mail: *chigochuck@aol.com*
Contact: Chuck Smith

The first prize for this competition is $2000! Transportation and housing are provided for the winner for a production. Second prize is $500 (and a staged reading), and the third prize is a staged reading at the Goodman Theater. You must be a United States resident of African-American descent. Your piece cannot have received a professional production. Write for guidelines (with SASE). The deadline for this contest is July 1, but please do not submit before April 1. The winners will be notified in November.

APPENDIX E

APPLYING FOR GRANTS

Another source of financial assistance for solo artists is grants. Most of the time, grants are authorized to institutions (such as theaters) rather than individual artists. The awards from the grants provide for commissions, development, and production costs.

Since most of the grants offer huge financial remuneration, attaining them can be quite competitive. I suggest that you apply as early as possible. If you have any questions or need advice regarding the grant, make sure to contact the organization directly. They can be very helpful in what is sometimes a complicated process. Do the best that you can in completing the application in an intelligent and thoughtful manner. Neatly type and answer all questions to the best of your ability. You are permitted to apply for as many grants as you wish, and I recommend that you do. You'll notice that once you have completed a grant proposal, it's not that difficult to adapt it for other grants.

- **Brody Arts Fund**
  California Community Foundation, 606 South Olive Street, Suite 2400, Los Angeles, CA 90014-1526, Tel. (213) 242-7489, Web site: *www.calfund.org*
  Contact: Program Secretary

  This foundation offers a $5000 fellowship. You must be a Los Angeles emerging artist in the "expansion arts." Expansion arts includes tribal, minority, rural, and inner city arts. You can apply in the spring for an application. It is available on a rotating basis to various other disciplines such as composers, screenwriters, etc. Contact the fund to find out if this is the appropriate time for solo artists. The deadline is March, but check to be sure. You'll be notified by June.

- **National Endowment for the Arts International Program**
1100 Pennsylvania Avenue NW, Room 618, Washington, DC 20506, Tel. (202) 682-5429, FAX (202) 682-5602, E-mail: *thefund@iie.org*   *Contact:* Pennie Ojeda

Arts Link Collaborative Projects
Send to CEC International Partners, 12 West 32nd Street, New York, NY 10001-4415, Tel. (212) 643-1985, FAX (212) 643-1996

Though most grants are between $1500 and $3500, they can be up to $6000. This grant is offered to U.S. artists to work with artists in the former Soviet Union, the Baltics, and Central and Eastern Europe in a mutually beneficial artistic collaboration. You must send a completed application and all other supporting material requested. The deadline is March 15. You'll hear back in a few months.

- **The Playwright's Center Grant Programs**
2301 Franklin Avenue East, Minneapolis, MN 55406-1099, Tel. (612) 332-7481, E-mail: *pwcenter@mtn.org,* Web site: *www.pwcenter.org*   *Contact:* Carlos Cuesta

The following grants and fellowships are offered through the Playwright's Center:

Jerome Playwright-in-Residence Fellowship
This annually offered fellowship offers five one-year fellowships of $7200. The Playwright's Center is looking for emerging artists (not more than two full productions of your work) willing to spend a year at the Center to develop their work. Send for SASE. The deadline is September 15. You'll be notified by January of the next year.

Many Voices Playwriting Residency Awards
This award is offered yearly (depending on availability of funds) to African-American residents of MN. The award is given to eight artists. It includes a $1000 stipend, a scholarship to playwriting classes, ongoing assistance by a dramaturge, and public readings. Send SASE for guidelines. The deadline for application is July 1. You'll be notified by September 15.

McKnight Advancement Grants
These yearly grants offer three awards of $8500. You must be a U.S. citizen and have been living in MN as a legal resident since May 1997. The grants are given to accomplished artists who have had at least two professional productions produced by a professional theater. The recipient must be willing to spend two months at the Center to participate in ongoing programs. Send SASE for guidelines. The deadline is February 1. You'll hear from the Center by May.

McKnight Fellowships
This annual fellowship awards two winners ten thousand dollars. The grant committee seeks accomplishment by the winning artist in contemporary theater. You must have had at least two fully produced productions of your work by a professional theater, and be willing to spend at least one month at the Center. The deadline for this fellowship is January 15. You'll be notified by April 15.

APPENDIX F

LITERARY AGENTS

Literary agents can be very helpful in getting your material to the best theaters (and the top readers) for your specific type of play. Although they primarily deal with regular plays, it's certainly worth your while to try and find an agent who believes in your monologue play.

It's been suggested that you should only contact a couple of agents at a time. Most literary agents request that you first send a query letter describing your piece. You should also enclose an updated bio with the letter and any press material or past reviews of your work. If you find a theater or club where you can perform your work, make sure that you contact any agents that have expressed interest in your work. For further information on finding the right literary agent for your material, contact:

- **The Association of Author's Representatives**
  10 Astor Place, 3rd Floor, New York, NY 10003

  Send the AAR a check or money order for $7 and a SASE (55¢) for its brochure.

LIST OF LITERARY AGENTS

- **Alan Brodie Representation Ltd.**
  211 Picadilly, London W1V 9LD England, Tel. 011-44-171-917-2871
  Contact: Alan Brodie or Sarah McNair

  They prefer recommendations by professionals known to their agency.

- **Alliance Talent Agency**
  1501 Broadway, Suite 404, New York, NY 10036, Tel. (212) 840-6868, FAX (212) 840-7237
  Contact: Carole Davis

  Send Carole Davis a copy of your monologue play or a synopsis and query letter.

- **Agency for the Performing Arts**
  888 7th Avenue, Suite 602, New York, NY 10106, Tel. (212) 582-1500   *Contact:* Leo Bookman

- **Ann Elmo Agency**
  60 East 42nd Street, New York, NY 10165, Tel. (212) 661-2800
  Contact: Mari Cronin or Letti Lee

- **Ann Wright Representatives**
  165 West 42nd Street, #1105, New York, NY 10036-2501, Tel. (212) 764-6770
  Contact: Dan Wright

  The representatives prefer that you send them a query letter with a SASE.

- **Barbara Hogenson Agency**
  165 West End Avenue, #19C, New York, NY 10023, Tel. (212) 874-8084, FAX (212) 362-3011
  Contact: Barbara Hogenson

- **Berman, Boals and Flynn, Inc.**
  225 Lafayette Street, Suite 1207, New York, NY 10012, Tel. (212) 966-0339
  Contact: Los Berman, Judy Boals, Jim Flynn

  They prefer that you make contact with them through one of their clients.

- **The Bethel Agency**
  360 West 53rd Street, Suite BA, New York, NY 10019, Tel. 664-0455
  Contact: Lewis Chambers

  Mr. Chambers prefers only query letters.

- **Bret Adams, Ltd.**
  448 West 44th Street, New York, NY 10036, Tel. (212) 765-5630, FAX (212) 265-2212
  Contact: Bret Adams, Bruce Ostler

- **Curtis Brown, Ltd.**
  28 Haymarket, London, SW1Y 4SP England, Tel. 011-44-171-396-6600, FAX 011-44-171-396-0110

  The agency prefers that you send your monologue play.

- **Don Buchwald and Associates**
  10 East 44th Street, New York, NY 10017, Tel. (212) 867-1200, FAX (212) 972-320
  Contact: Theatrical Department

  A query or synopsis along with a bio is preferred.

- **Douglas, Gorman, Rothacker and Wilhelm**
  1501 Broadway, Suite 703, New York, NY 10036, Tel. (212) 382-2000, FAX (212) 719-2878

  Send them ten pages of your monologue, a résumé, and a query letter.

• **Duva-Flack Associates, Inc.**
200 West 57th Street, Suite 1008, New York, NY 10019, Tel. (212) 957-9600, FAX (212) 957-9606

• **Flora Roberts**
157 West 57th Street, New York, NY 10019, Tel. (212) 355-4165, FAX (212) 246-7138
Contact: Flora Roberts, Sarah Douglas

They are looking for playwrights with outstanding credits. Send a query with a résumé.

• **The Gersh Agency**
130 West 42nd Street, Suite 2400, New York, NY 10036, Tel. (212) 997-1818, FAX (212) 391-8459
Contact: Peter Hagen

The Gersh Agency prefers a professional recommendation or a query letter with SASE.

• **The Graham Agency**
311 West 43rd Street, New York, NY 10036, Tel. (212) 489-7730
Contact: Earl Graham

• **Helen Merril, Ltd.**
425 West 23rd Street, Suite 1F, New York, NY 10011, Tel. (212) 691-5326
Contact: Patrick Herold

• **Impulse Dramatists**
3131 S.W. Sherwood Place, Portland, OR 97201-2254
Contact: Ed Udovick

Ed Udovick accepts unsolicited scripts.

• **International Creative Management**
40 West 57th Street, New York, NY 10019, Tel. (212) 556-5600
Contact: Bridget Aschenberg, Sam Cohn, Arlene Donovan, Mitch Douglas

• **The Joyce Ketay Agency**
1501 Broadway, Suite 1908, New York, NY 10036, Tel. (212) 354-6825, FAX (212) 354-6732,
E-mail: *ketay@aol.com*   *Contact:* Joyce Ketay, Carl Mulert, Wendy Streeter

They prefer you to contact them only through referrals.

• **The Lantz Office**
888 7th Avenue, #2500, New York, NY 10106, Tel. (212) 586-0200
Contact: Robert Lantz, Dennis Aspland

• **Literary Artists Representatives**
575 West End Avenue, New York, NY 10024, (212) 787-3808, FAX (212) 595-2098
Contact: Madeline Perrone

• **Peregrine Whittlesey Agency**
345 East 80th Street, #31F, New York, NY 10021, Tel. (212) 737-0153, FAX (212) 734-5176
Contact: Peregrine Whittlesey

Peregrine Whittlesey prefers that you send a query with résumé. It is looking only for "original writing."

- **Rosenstone/Wender**
  3 East 48th Street, New York, NY 10017, Tel. (212) 832-8330, FAX (212) 759-4524
  Contact: Ron Gwiazda, Howard Rosenstone, Phyllis Wender

- **The Shukat Company**
  340 West 55th Street, Suite 1A, New York, NY 10019-3744, Tel. (212) 582-7614,
  E-mail: *staff@shukat.com*

- **Susan Shulman Literary Agency**
  454 West 44th Street, New York, NY 10036, Tel. (212) 713-1633, FAX (212) 581-8830,
  E-mail: *schulman@aol.com*   *Contact:* Susan Schulman

  Susan prefers a professional recommendation or a query letter.

- **Talent Representatives**
  20 East 53rd Street, Suite 2A, New York, NY 10022, Tel. (212) 752-1835, FAX (212) 752-7558
  Contact: Honey Raider

- **The Tantleff Agency**
  375 Greenwich Street, #700, New York, NY 10013, Tel. (212) 941-3939, FAX (212) 941-3948
  Contact: Jack Tantleff, Charmaine Ferenczi

- **Writers and Artists Agency**
  19 West 44th Street, Suite 1000, New York, NY 10036, Tel. (212) 391-1112, FAX (212) 575-6397
  Contact: William Craver, Greg Wagner

  They prefer that you don't send your queries by fax.

- **Greg Ziegler**
  160 East 97th Street, New York, NY 10029

  Greg Ziegler prefers that you send a synopsis with a short sample of your monologue and a query letter.

Permissions

Spalding Gray
Excerpt from *Swimming to Cambodia*, ©1985 by Spalding Gray. Published by Theater Communications Group, Inc., 355 Lexington Avenue, New York, N.Y. 10017. Reprinted by permission of the author.

Excerpt from *Gray's Anatomy*, ©1993 by Spalding Gray. Published by Vintage Books, a division of Random House, Inc. Reprinted by permission of the author.

Evan Handler
Excerpt from *Time On Fire*, ©1996 by Evan Handler. Published by Little Brown & Company Limited. Reprinted by permission of the author.

Sherry Glaser
Excerpt from *Oh My Goddess*, ©1998 by Sherry Glaser. Reprinted by permission of the author.

Charlayne Woodard
Excerpt from *Pretty Fire*, by Charlayne Woodard. Published by Penguin Press. Permission granted by the author.

Shelly Mars
Excerpt from *An Evening with Shelly Mars*. Reprinted by permission granted by the author.

ABOUT THE AUTHOR

Glenn Alterman is the author of *Street Talk: Original Character Monologues for Actors, Uptown: More Original Character Monologues for Actors, Two Minutes and Under, The Job Book: One Hundred Acting Jobs for Actors, The Job Book 2: One Hundred Day Jobs for Actors, What to Give Your Agent for Christmas: And 100 Other Helpful Hints for Working Actors, Promoting Your Acting Career,* and *Two Minute Monologs.*

Street Talk and *Uptown* were the number one best-selling books of original monologues in 1992 and 1993. *The Job Book, The Job Book 2, Two Minutes and Under,* and *What to Give Your Agent* . . . were featured selections in The Doubleday Book Club (Fireside Theater and Stage and Screen divisions). *Street Talk, Two Minutes and Under,* and *100 Acting Jobs* . . . are presently in their second printing.

His plays *Like Family* and *The Pecking Order* were optioned by Red Eye Films (with Alterman writing the screenplay).

Nobody's Flood won the Bloomington National Playwriting Competition and was a finalist in The Key West Playwriting Competition. *Coulda-Woulda-Shoulda* won The Three Genres Playwriting Competition (including publication of the play in the Prentice Hall college textbook). He wrote the book *Heartstrings—The National Tour* (commissioned by the Design Industries Foundation for AIDS), a thirty-five city tour, which starred Michelle Pfeiffer, Ron Silver, Christopher Reeve, Susan Sarandon, Marlo Thomas, and Sandy Duncan.

Other plays include *Kiss Me When It's Over* (commissioned by E. Weissman Productions) starring and directed by Andre DeShields, *Tourists of the Mindfield* (finalist in the L. Arnold Weissberger Playwriting Competition at New Dramatists), and *Street Talk/Uptown,* the play based on his books, produced at The West Coast Ensemble in Los Angeles. *Goin' Round on Rock Solid Ground* and *Unfamiliar Faces* were finalists at the Actor's Theater of Louisville. *Spilt Milk* received its premiere at the Beverly Hills Rep/Theater 40 in Los Angeles and was selected to participate in The Samuel French One-Act Festival. *The Danger of Strangers* won Honorable Mention in both The Deep South Writers Conference Competition and the Pittsburgh New Works Festival, and was also a finalist in the George R. Kernodle Contest (with subsequent productions at Circle Rep Lab and The West Bank Downstairs Theater Bar).

His plays have also been performed in New York at Primary Stages, Circle in the Square Downtown, at the HERE theater, at LaMama, in the Turnip Festival, at the Duplex, Playwrights Horizons, on several theaters on Theater Row, at the John Drew Theater in East Hampton, New York, and at many other theaters around the country.

Mr. Alterman is a member of the Dramatists Guild, The National Writers Union, The Author's Guild, The Participating Artists at The Cherry Lane Theater, Circle Rep Lab, The 42nd Street Workshop, and The Lab Theater Company.

He has taught original monologue writing classes at The Lab Theater Company and in private classes in New York and Los Angeles.

INDEX

Books from Allworth Press

Promoting Your Acting Career by Glenn Alterman (softcover, 6 × 9, 224 pages, $18.95)

Technical Theater for Nontechnical People by Drew Campbell (softcover, 6 × 9, 256 pages, $18.95)

An Actor's Guide—Your First Year in Hollywood by Michael Saint Nicholas (softcover, 6 × 9, 256 pages, $16.95)

Selling Scripts to Hollywood by Katherine Atwell Herbert (softcover, 6 × 9, 176 pages, $12.95)

The Sreenwriter's Legal Guide, Second Edition by Stephen F. Breimer (softcover, 6 × 9, 320 pages, $19.95)

Writing Scripts Hollywood Will Love by Katherine Atwell Herbert (softcover, 6 × 9, 160 pages, $12.95)

Booking and Tour Management for the Performing Arts by Rena Shagan (softcover, 6 × 9, 272 pages, $19.95)

Stage Fright: Health and Safety in the Theater by Monona Rossol (softcover, 6 × 9, 144 pages, $16.95)

Writing Television Comedy by Jerry Rannow (softcover, 6 × 9, 224 pages, $14.95)

Money Secrets of the Rich and Famous by Michael Reynard (hardcover, 6¼ × 9¼, 256 pages, $24.95)

Please write to request our free catalog. To order by credit card, call 1-800-491-2808 or send a check or money order to Allworth Press, 10 East 23rd Street, Suite 210, New York, NY 10010. Include $5 for shipping and handling for the first book ordered and $1 for each additional book. Ten dollars plus $1 for each additional book if ordering from Canada. New York State residents must add sales tax.

To see our complete catalog on the World Wide Web, or to order online, you can find us at *www.allworth.com*.